# A Horse in My Kit Bag

# A Horse
# in My Kit Bag

## Olga Pyne Clarke

Methuen . London

First published in Great Britain 1988
by Methuen London Limited
11 New Fetter Lane, London EC4P 4EE
Copyright © 1988 Olga Pyne Clarke

Printed in Great Britain
by Redwood Burn Ltd,
Trowbridge, Wiltshire

---

British Library Cataloguing in Publication Data

Clarke, Olga Pyne, *1915–*
A horse in my kit bag.
1. Western Europe. Social life, 1939–1945.
Personal observations
I. Title
940.53′092′4

ISBN 0-413-17400-X

---

# CONTENTS

# ILLUSTRATIONS

The author the day before war was declared
18 Pioneer Corps at Tessenderloo, 1944
Captain Frank Conway-Upton
Major Charles Beach
Colonel Fritz Renton
Lt. Colonel Ray Mumford ('Tiger Tim')
The original Old One-Two sign
27 CRASC at Freistett, 1945
The three-hare window, Paderborn
Hermione Wolf
The author in 1949
Vanessa in Helsinki, 1950
Vanessa giving a press conference
The Guernica oak leaf
At a charity ball, 1962
Erna aged 22
Erna aged 24
The author and Scali Rua, 1969
The author and Miss Rafferty, 1982

# FOREWORD

This book follows my first book of autobiography, *She Came of Decent People*, about my childhood in Ireland and my life up to the start of the Second World War. As in that book, for personal reasons I have altered the names of some of the leading personalities.

Forty years takes toll of one's memory, so if there are minor discrepancies in the war chapters I ask the readers to forgive them. All my notebooks, diaries, precious letters and photographs sent to my late father for safe-keeping were burned after his death when our old home was sold (which is why I have no photographs of either Guy or Vandy). The few documents that have survived accidentally were omitted from the Deed Box, remaining in my own files.

To the following people I owe a very big debt of gratitude: Isobel Hinshelwood and Ian Stuttard of Thames Television, who spurred me into writing my first book; Gwen Conway-Upton, who lent me Frank's notes and did research for me; Diana Condell of the Imperial War Museum, who never failed to answer the most trivial question; Pauline Hallam, the French Tourist Public Relations Officer; Major E. R. Elliott, Pioneer Corps Ret'd.; Colonel P. M. J. Harrison OBE, MC; and Hermoine Waller, who all helped to fit some of the missing pieces into place; Andree Dorrington-Ward, who still wrestles uncomplainingly after three years with my appalling writing and mis-spelling; Patrick and Angela McCarthy for their practical and general help in photocopying the manuscript for the publishers; Corporal A. D. Gratten, RE, for providing a copy of the Corps Song; and, not least, Ann Mansbridge of Methuen for her kindness, helpful understanding and support.

Dedicated in affectionate memory to my father,
Ernest Pyne Clarke,
and Cousins Jack and Millicent Jackson.

'They took their fence daily,
Boldly and gaily;
With never a falter,
Rode straight to the end.'

# — 1 —

# Initial Training

The Second World War left but few families in England without bereavement. For my case, in April 1942 it took a very much loved mother-in-law and our mutual home in the West Country, and three months later my adored husband, Guy. To know that you are only one of thousands is not much solace, but it gives you some awareness of other people's sorrows. I wanted to do something for the soldiers who were giving their all for us, yet keep the promise I gave Guy, not to join any of the women's services. After careful thought, I settled for the YMCA, the largest organisation in the Council of Voluntary War Workers under which all voluntary organisations were grouped. As my parents were still obdurate in not accepting my marriage, always writing to me as Miss Clarke, I took the line of least resistance and joined under my maiden name. Before doing so, however, I wanted to get a basic knowledge of how real army welfare worked. The polite type of troop welfare that went with being a Colonel's lady in peacetime would not be sufficient to make one confident of dealing with the fighting men away from their homes and families with all the strains of war pressing on them.

So in September 1943 I appealed to a trusted army friend, who suggested he had just the job for me, with an irascible Irish sapper major, Chipps Woodley, Deputy Command Royal Engineers (DCRE) at Attleborough in Norfolk. He was a demon to work for, would not have a male driver, and no ATS would drive him owing to his abusiveness during his drinking bouts. The latter were caused by his bronchial troubles, only giving temporary relief, then making matters worse.

Underlying all this, he had, when sober, a heart of pure gold. He, I was told by the CRE, Colonel Villiers, would be instructed that he was to teach me the real meaning of welfare in return for getting a

9

civilian driver/dogsbody. My main duty was to keep Chipps out of the pubs at night and to sit him down to his drawing board after dinner when the rest of the staff had left. I fetched him from his billet to the office at 7.15 pm and delivered him back when he had finished his stint of cartography on rice-paper. The rest of the staff did not like my presence, since Chipps took me to any social function he was invited to (albeit he always, after chewing his immediate aides up in small pieces for a week, would take them to lunch and a matinee, or dinner and a show, in Cambridge to make amends). He instilled his motto into me: 'A good officer looks after all his men, but to do this properly he must look after himself.'

Working with Chipps was like reading a very bizarre novel or sitting on a 'time-bomb with the pin drawn'. No two days ran smoothly, but he was a born teacher, and what a brain! Some of the extraneous things he taught me – to read upside-down papers from the other side of the desk; never to give a soldier legal advice but to tell him which officer to contact, or go to the said officer yourself; court all your immediate officers who in civilian life were bankers, solicitors, estate agents and of course your padre, but, in Chipps's words, 'Make sure he's not a Holy Joe idiot.' – stood me in good stead not only during but after the war.

Chipps's brand of English was extraordinary. Born of top-brass Irish gentry, he had been stationed in Yorkshire for a long time and also sent on special missions to Mexico and France. He did his calculations aloud in either pure Parisian French or Mexican Spanish, and when in a rage, cursed and swore in the broadest of broad Yorkshire, his 'aitches' flying around like wasps whose nest had been upset. He never tired of sniping at me about Vandy Cunningham,\* now a half-Colonel and stationed outside Newmarket. Not yet back on the active service list owing to a badly smashed leg in Dunkirk, he had quite a bit of free time, often coming up for a weekend. He had moved into my old billet in Snailwell Rectory and had become great friends with those two dear people the Reverend George and Etta Purdue, as indeed had Chipps, who knew many of

---

\* Vandy Cunningham had made his home with my Kildare cousins for over twenty years, and being twelve years older than me, was like an older brother or young uncle. He was also my late husband's lifelong friend and partner in their horses. (See *She Came of Decent People*.)

their friends and relations in Ireland. But for all his sniping and leg-pulling, whenever possible Chipps included Vandy in all his parties, whether shooting, dinner or theatre.

Another of Chipps's friends was a Canadian doctor, Etienne du Croix, one of the few to survive the shameful Dieppe débâcle of August 1942. His Forestry Company HQ was a delightful small manor house between Thetford and Brandon. Its owner, Colonel Gurney, was a retired Indian Army officer whose wife was a New Zealander. Their family consisted of a son at Lancing College and a daughter, the latter being with them in New Zealand when war broke out. The estate was small, consisting of a home farm with nicely laid-out grounds and stabling and a tenant farm of about 200 acres. The tenant farmer was a very surly chap, always making trouble for the agent and us about the Canadians. We often went to jolly parties in that manor house, though we never met the owners as they were marooned in New Zealand, and the boy spent his holidays with someone near Brandon.

Little did I dream the degradation and misery this house was inadvertently to cause me in years to come.

Etienne du Croix could manage Chipps, treating him for his chest troubles. He was not like Chipps's description of our own Army Medical Officers as 'stoopid boogers who'd spin ya for ya wind and have a chap out on his arse before e'd know where e'd bin'. Chipps lived in dread of being invalided out: he need not have worried, the work he was doing was much too important.

It was during these evening sessions that I drew first blood at getting into print. *Horse and Hound* paid me ten shillings for a poem called 'The Exile', which was reprinted in the *Daily Sketch*, and the *Newmarket Journal* five shillings and six pence for doggerel verses on the DCRE.

### The Exile

How I long to be in Ireland when the winter comes again,
To hear the patter of the Hounds' feet and soft west Rain,
Hear the shuffle of the Asses with their loaded Creels of turf –
And the crash upon the shingle of the Broad Atlantic surf.

The Packs may be cut down to half, and the horses clipped trace high
But you know that they can gallop –
When the Hounds are in full cry.
With the West Wind blowing the clouds off Galteemore,
And the ragged barefoot urchins clinging round the cottages' half door.

The fields they are depleted more than many people know –
To answer England's Call to Arms the youngsters were not slow –
Ireland gave, as usual, all her daughters and her sons –
To be butchered by the Japanese and slaughtered by the Huns.

You would not guess the sorrow of the older Hunting crowd
For they still go as hard as ever and are in their trial proud,
Thinking of the Hunts now past, their sons, how well they went –
Perhaps now lying wounded in some swelt'ring Burmese Tent.

T'was Fox Hunting that made them the Soldiers that they are,
And taught them how to lead their men quite fearlessly in War.
The Master jogging on in front thinks of a war long gone
And of his scattered comrades – their heirs now fighting on.

There's not a bank or open ditch that could not tell a tale
From the famous Cryhelp Country down to the Golden Vale –
Now of some hunting incident or yet some favourite's skill,
How Mick got jumped off Starlight or Eamon lept the Moy on little Silver
　　Grill.

The Pack crash into Sprats Town and the Fox is viewed away,
So tight'ning girths and short'ning reins, aside our thoughts we lay.
Now hustling up the Bowery Bog and lepping into Usk
Until along the old Bog road we homeward jog at dusk.

'Tis then the ghosts come back once more, and ride with us again.
As the mists steal up from Narraghmore with just a hint of rain.
How I'd love to see the Hill of Allen and the Chair of Old Kildare,
To ride with Guy, and talk to him, and see the sunset on his hair.

To keep the Pack together when they try to break away,
For Horse and Hound and Boy and Man have had enough today.
Once again the old familiar scene of waving sterns I see –
Wishing I was jogging home to Fairview, hot cakes and talk and tea.


## The Lament of Timothy
### (With apologies to A. A. Milne)

The Assistant lay there in her little camp bed
Feeling so sick with a very fat head.
She turned over to shut out the sight
of Pioneers Black and Sappers white.

Romney, Iris and Nissen Huts
Simply sent the poor girl nuts.
Bricks and concrete – Bits, Braces and Dyes:
She clenched up fists and shut up her eyes.

The MO came bustling and breezy and kind,
The Major came swearing and wheezing behind.
The MO stood frowning and shaking his head:
He took up his fore-and-aft cap as he said:
'What the patient requires is a change,' and he went
To see about posting her down South to Kent.

The Assistant sat up and said with a sigh,
'I suppose all these people know better than I:
It is silly perhaps, but I really would like
To ride horses again, and not just a BIKE.'

The MO said, 'Tut, it's another attack,'
And ordered her milk and massage of the back,
Pictures and dances and Drives in a car:
He murmured 'How sweet these dear Sapper boys are.'

The Assistant sat there with her fists in her eyes
And imagined herself such a lovely surprise
Of soft West winds and Irish skies,
And a cock-tailed horse, sure-footed and wise.

This tale is of Timothy, who drove a tiny Austin flea
And helped a crusty old DCRE,
Who filled in forms, and inspected drains,
Missed the buses, and caught the trains.

He wrote in a book called 412,
All about something that nobody knew:
And lots of vouchers AB 43,
Signed with a flourish – Major, RE

After I had been at Attleborough for a while, a dreadful row blew up over requisition of land between the Air Ministry and the DCRE's Department, the former saying that the DCRE had requisitioned what was theirs. Three VIPs were sent, armed with capacious files, maps, map references etc., to do battle on the site. It so happened that Chipps, who had an important conference with the American hierarchy, could not get away, and it fell to my lot to take them and Willie, our civilian Clerk of Works, who was only just out of a sick bed and suffering from a heart condition.

We all packed into the staff car, getting to the site at noon. The field in question had about six yearling heifers in it – wild horses would not get our heroes out of the car until the 'bulls' were driven away. Having cleared the decks, we all got out our maps. I had Chipps's, Willie had his own Ordnance Survey maps of the exact spot: there was great murmuring and consultation between the three guests. Willie glanced at their map, thinking it was upside down, and taking a closer look he found it to be of another area, much nearer Ipswich and not in our jurisdiction. They ranted and raved that they had been given the wrong maps. We then asked to see the files, which were indeed for a site near Ipswich.

They then demanded lunch, so we took them to the Bell in Bury St Edmunds. As we were going in with them, they told us to wait in the car. I ignored them. Seeing Willie looking a bit blue round the mouth, I took him to the bar and gave him a brandy. Like the 'Three Jolly Huntsmen', the Men from the Ministry 'munched and they gobbled' until nearly 3.30 pm, and then demanded to be taken to Norwich to see about the mistake. I got a lift home for poor Willie, keeping his notes and maps with me. What they got up to in Norwich no one knows, but at 5 pm they ordered me to take them straight back to the Air Ministry in Newmarket.

We were just outside Norwich when the crash warning went. It was against orders to move a military vehicle whilst a raid was on, especially at night, so I made tracks for a King's Own Yorkshire Light Infantry Personnel Holding Unit just down the road. But within 800 yards of the entrance, bang! went a back tyre. The language and abuse I got from the three gents was nobody's business. Could I get them out of the car to jack it up and change the tyre? No way. The three of them sat like stuffed, very frightened monkeys in the back, holding their briefcases over their heads. We were between two ack-ack batteries and there was a fair bit of flak about. The search lights helped me to see what I was doing, but I did not make haste as it was interesting to see Jerry caught in the beams like a fly in amber. The jack was of the ratchet type, very worn, and each time I got it to the required height the weight of the gents was too much – it gave up the unequal struggle, crashing down again.

I was on the point of walking off to the KOYLI outfit for help when a large figure loomed out of the night and in broad Yorkshire asked, 'What's up, sonny?' He made a few pertinent, well-chosen remarks about real gentlemen and told me to go with him, taking the keys and the rotor arm. We abandoned the car with its contents. He was the biggest Company Sergeant Major I have ever seen, and I felt like a Shetland pony cantering to keep up with a Shire horse. In the guard room he called for the Duty Officer, a poor little chap of about 19 years, very newly commissioned, whose terror of the CSM was only equalled by that of me. In stentorian tones the CSM told him to take the lady to the Adjutant: – 'Sah, tell him she is in trouble, Sah! and that she is the DCRE's assistant and the lady wot shoots, Sah!' Every time he said 'Sah', one got the impression that the single pips on the poor little chap's shoulders covered their eyes, peering out through their fingers, and his Adam's apple did a double flip on its trampoline. Poor young man, he raced me to the Adjutant's office, repeated verbatim the CSM's instructions, saluted and bolted. I did look a fearsome sight, mud and grease on my face, muddy knees and mud in my hair.

The Adjutant was made of sterner stuff and put me through on the telephone to Chipps. The bellow as to why I was not back reverberated round the room. Being told of the puncture and where I was, he calmed down a little, but when I told him why we were late arriving, owing to the Bull episode, all hell was let loose. I had to hold the phone at arm's length. 'I'll Bull the b—s when you get back, Group their Captains for them . . .' after which he succinctly traced their ancestry back to the primaeval slime without benefit of clergy! I could hear poor Potty, Chipps's secretary, chuckling, then in dulcet tones Chipps asked the Adjutant if they could get me some refreshments while someone was repairing the tyre. Having cleaned up again, and been given a few drinks and sandwiches, I was told by the Adjutant that all was ready; the 'gentlemen' had been kept in the guard room.

I was met by a volley of abuse from them as they got into the car and was told to drive like hell as they would be late for their dinner appointment in Newmarket. Saying nothing, I drove quietly back to HQ, took the car keys and reported to Chipps, who kept them waiting half an hour whilst I got a rocket and had a day's leave docked for moving an army vehicle in a raid. He then sent our staff corporal to collect them, and gave them hell's own dressing down, telling them they could find their own way back to Newmarket. What I did not know until afterwards was that the Adjutant had phoned up an adverse report of their abuse to me and their bad behaviour in the guard room.

Later I found out that the CSM was the son of a gamekeeper and had seen Chipps and me potting the odd pheasant from the 'Flea' (our Austin 7) when on the battle school, the live ammunition training ground at Thetford. Also it was he who had reported the Group Captains' bad behaviour to the Adjutant.

With everyone working full stretch in the war effort, I was appalled at the attitude of the civilian Ministry officials, of which this incident was a typical example. Mostly able-bodied men of serviceable age in reserved occupations, their pettiness, in-fighting and pomposity, coupled with their muddles, cost the country dear in terms of wasted time and manpower.

# 2

# NORFOLK

After I had been working for him for about six weeks, Chipps suddenly went to town on me – nothing was right – so when Potty was out of the office I let fly at him. It was a mean thing to do, for as I was a civilian, he had no jurisdiction over me, nor could he put me on a 'phizzer', *but* it had the desired effect. He asked Etienne, Mrs Baise (head of Impressed), Vandy, Potty and me to dinner and the theatre the following Saturday. The play was *The Man Who Came to Dinner* with the original cast.

Whilst waiting in the theatre foyer for Chipps, who was talking to an American officer, a tribe, (which is all I could call them) trooped in led by a gaunt woman with a pallid face and sunken, burning eyes, dressed in high fashion of the mid-twenties, walking with a peculiar flat-footed, knee-pumping action. After her trooped five daughters, all spotty, chinless and beaky-nosed, looking half-starved and with the same period of dress and way of walking. The rear of this flotilla was brought up by a short, pink, cubistic man: everything about him was square, even to his blonde head, face and moustache.

The lady halted in front of Etienne. 'How nice to meet you again: do introduce me to Colonel – ah, haven't we met before?'

'No', said Vandy, firmly turning away.

Etienne grinned at her, saying, 'You would not know him, he's in the IRA.' She too moved off.

Apparently she was Lady Petronella Pinchingham, known locally, we were to discover, as 'Pet the Pinch', and she was notorious for husband-hunting among the senior ranks for her spotty brood. Etienne put us all in the picture over supper. She had invited all the officers in the district of field rank and above to her famous weekends, either for shooting or tennis. None would ever repeat the ordeal.

Shortly after this our HQ was joined by a very nice American Liaison Officer, Major Wesley Orr. He was a charming man, an excellent shot as well as being an authority on heavy draught horses. He looked prim, but had such a twinkle in his eye: even Chipps failed to shock him. He had been a New York architect and, like Chipps, was terrific to go about with as their knowledge of buildings was profound. We had in our area many of the great houses of the eastern counties, and it was an education to listen to the two of them.

*The* invitation came at the end of November: 'Would Major Woodley care to come for a shooting weekend to Pinchingham Park and bring Colonel Cunningham, Major Orr and his driver.'

'My word,' said Etienne, 'you *are* honoured, but *don't* be fooled, she wants you as a beater.'

Chipps said, 'Let's go for the giggle,' but taking Etienne's advice, we went well armed with food and extra bedding. The American Hospital was one of our 'babies', so we had access to the PX (the American equivalent of the NAAFI).

We arrived at 'Do the Boys' Park as instructed for tea on Friday afternoon. Our fellow guest was a very famous impresario who for politic reasons I will not name, but he was Pet's Cher Ami. Her cubistic husband was called Paul and all the spotty offspring's names began with P – Patricia, Pauline, Priscilla, Perdita and Prudence. Mats and rugs scattered round the house had the cypher of entwined 'Ps'.

The tea was so weak it could hardly creep out of the pot. There was no sugar and if you took it, only a tiny jug of milk. A small head of gritty lettuce in a greasy bowl, a thin slice of stale bread each and a communal tiny pat of margarine – and *that* was our tea.

'Johnny Dear', the impresario, sat next to Pet, who patted his hand and urged him to eat up. He had butter, two scones, jam and his private jug of milk. He was a tall, thin, grey man with a faraway vacant look in his eyes, which for all that were hooded and mighty shrewd. His colour scheme was grey, like his face and hair. Pet was stage-struck and I think she fancied herself as a second Ottoline Morrell, but certainly without the panache.

After tea we were shown to our rooms. Vandy had a room to himself with a wash-basin; the other two had to share. I was put right away in an unused wing smelling of mice and cold as charity. The three came down to my quarters, bringing their food and drink with them. We had a few before dinner, which consisted of a brace of pheasant (after the soup, which was obviously cabbage water), a bowl of nasty soapy potatoes on the table and another of over-cooked Brussels sprouts, all for twelve people. There was no fire in the dining room and just a drugget on the floor. Johnny Dear had a breast of one of the pheasants. We had a good imitation of the Irish peasants' 'potatoes and point'. (In the bad old days they hung a bloater over the table and all the family wiped their potatoes against it, the little ones who couldn't reach only pointing at it, hence the expression.) For pudding, a jar of badly discoloured home-preserved raspberries – *that* was our lot. We repaired to the gun room as it was small and did not take so much heating: it really took none at all because the fire of damp logs only sent hissing smoke up the chimney. We were repeatedly told it was war-time, so we had to go to bed at 10 pm because the Lister engine which made the light was stopped by then. Chipps and Vandy kicked up at where I was quartered but were smartly told, 'But, Major Woodley, she is only your driver, with no rank. She will get warm tomorrow, beating.'

'That,' said Chipps and Vandy as one man, 'she will *not* do. She was invited to shoot, and is as good a shot as anyone.' Very rude of them, but in the circumstances, justifiable. Poor Pet was very upset.

We had a lovely midnight feast provided from the PX: a tin of ham, water biscuits, tins of fruit with Carnation milk washed down with either whisky or beer. There were notices in the bathroom reminding us that owing to war conditions the hot taps did not work, and the bath had the regulation four-inch Plimsoll line painted on it. I had to trail about half a mile through corridors to get to the one allocated to us, all other doors in my wing being locked.

Breakfast was lumpy, watery porridge, well salted, dandelion coffee, one slice of cold toast assisted by a very thin substance purported to be marmalade. Johnny Dear had his breakfast in bed. The five siblings, looking blue with cold, hugged their poor flat bosoms with goose pimpled arms, keeping up a kind of neighing dog language giggle. They ranged in age from about 15 to 25, the youngest being, I think, slightly subnormal and the one Pet had destined for the theatre. After a squealed giggle, one or other of them would say to whoever sat next to her: 'I'm laughing at – , she's farting again, she's so naughty!' Once or twice I caught Vandy's or Chipps's eye, and we nearly succumbed to gigglement as well.

The first stand of the shoot was in a kale field; and to get to it we had to go through the farmyard. There was every conceivable type of domestic bird, suitable for either table or egg production, two pigs and a large stall of cows being milked by hand. The dairy door was open and an old crone was churning – so why the scarcity of food?

The partridge were of the French variety and well driven by the five girls, who to keep them at home were supposed to work on the farm. I was given the end stand: it so happened it was the best, the way the birds were coming over, and I got two brace. The next beat was a turnip field: the boys did very well, but nothing came over me. We walked about a mile to the next – very poor results – then Pet came out with lunch, with the gamekeeper and Johnny Dear in a donkey cart. They then collected the morning's bag whilst we sat on rugs for lunch. To see Pet and Johnny Dear sitting in the cart clutching a huge basket sent Chipps, Vandy and me into hysterics.

'All she wants,' said Chipps, 'is a bit of straw, and a shawl with the pig tied in the crib, then you could sing "The Low Back Car".'

The large 'game pie' was rabbit, with no eggs in it. Johnny Dear had a tot of gin and a leg of chicken. Sitting there with his long grey face, Lloyd Georgian hair, grey trilby hat turned down all round, the collar of his grey tweed coat turned up, he looked as if he had materialised out of a Norfolk fog. Suddenly, waving his half-eaten drumstick in the air, he began to declaim Noel Coward's topical, much-quoted poem, 'Lie in the Dark and Listen'. His perfect diction and sonorous tones held us all spellbound. Noel Coward or Michael MacLiammóir could not have bettered it.

After the lunch we walked up our birds ourselves as the young ladies had jobs to do at home. The bag was poor: Vandy bagged a pheasant, Chipps a snipe and a woodcock, and Wesley a brace of duck, so all in all we all got something. On returning to the house, Chipps asked to see the bag, as was usual, but was smartly told it had been taken direct to the station for a poulterer in Cambridge. Cold and dispirited, we made tracks for our quarters, looking forward to our own liquid refreshment. Chipps had his special strong peppermints and a bottle of gin as well as half a bottle of whisky – or so he thought. Wesley had six cans of beer, a tin of spam and a long carton of Camel cigarettes. Vandy, like me, had left his suitcase locked. We had between us a bottle of cherry brandy, half a bottle of ordinary brandy and the remains of last night's whisky. I also had the rest of our tin of ham and water biscuits.

They all descended on me: cigarettes, spam, gin and peppermints were gone. Was I playing a joke? Then Vandy asked if I'd taken his after-shave lotion. He and my Cousin Jack always used a rather expensive French one which had the nice tangy smell one gets when passing an apple orchard in bloom in the early morning. I used to sluice myself with it as a small child; to deter me they told me I would grow a beard! As we commiserated, I looked at my dressing-table and to my horror saw that my big box of Morny talcum powder plus swansdown puff were gone: it was practically unobtainable, but Vandy had brought it back from Dublin as a birthday present for me. We were all raging. On his way back to his room, Chipps got a hunch to search a housemaids' pantry near it. The empty spam tin and three beer cans were in it, and in the cupboard were the three remaining cans of beer and about a quarter of the bottle of gin, all of which he retrieved.

Not being able to stand another night, we laid a plan that friends of Vandy's, with whom we were going to stay on the Sunday, should ring up at decent intervals, Mrs Barton first pretending to be Mrs Baise demanding Chipps's immediate return owing to something blowing up, and her husband for Vandy to return to Soham as something had occurred that needed him urgently. As we were drinking our weak tea, Wesley made a great to-do about not having any cigarettes and could he get them at the local?

We decided we would have the calls put through during dinner. The simple sister was smothered in my powder, the second one was drunk as an owl and the eldest, slightly tipsy, stank of after-shave lotion and strong peppermints! At the local the landlord asked Wesley and Chipps if they had come from the park for a warm-up and something to eat, as guests usually did, leaving that night. We discussed how right Etienne's warning had been, and when we got to the Bartons at Swaffham they put us further in the picture. Chipps and Wesley got rooms at the Bull at Barton Mills. So all in all, if we had a night's discomfort and were not given a share of our endeavours, at least we got a laugh.

After the war, the poor cubistic husband had an accident in the gun room, blowing his brains out. Pet then married Johnny Dear, who only survived a couple of years.

The civilian staff at Attleborough loathed me. The ringleader was a blonde of doubtful age who suffered with the 'nerves', always getting a 'fright', flapping and squawking like a white Leghorn pullet if anyone followed her up the stairs or along the corridor. Mrs Baise got very fed up with her tears and 'vapourings', as she called them. She kept Chipps and Potty well informed about the Leghorn's whispered innuendoes.

Mrs Baise knew I was there for a specific purpose and may or may not have known what Chipps did in the evenings. The rest of them would have been very disappointed had they seen what went on. An old wheezy major bent over his drawing-board muttering and cursing to himself in French or Spanish, his assistant reading, playing patience, writing articles about the ghost-invaded Fenlands or knitting interminable sleeves, collars and cuffs for leather jerkins, made up by Mrs Nursey's famous leather shop in Bungay. This knitting would eventually earn me a three-quarter-length sheepskin coat. Some evenings Etienne would wander in to check on Chipps's wheeze.

Our after-dinner sessions lasted from approximately 7 to 9 pm. When I made Chipps tea, allowing him a drop of rum in it, Etienne said it would help him to sleep. Having discovered I could play bezique Etienne and I would play with makeshift markers until tea-time. Sometimes Chipps would join in, and like my notorious great-great aunt, Kate Pearson, make his own rules, which were a bit 'off-putting'. Then I took him back to his billet and so ended the evening sessions.

After a few weeks of this, finding I could not sleep and missing the great outdoors, I volunteered to drive a tea-car three nights a week from Norwich round the outlying ack-ack batteries. By running like mad after bringing the car back to base, I could just catch the 9.35 train to Norwich. The GI Passion Wagon would bring me back at midnight from St Peter Mancroft in Norwich. It dropped me within a mile of the town and I was back in the Angel, the pub where I was billeted, by 1 am. Mrs Baise and my landlady were the only ones who knew of this for safety reasons in case there was an air raid.

This worked well for six weeks until the Leghorn got hold of it, or part of it. Her telling Mrs Baise I was a security risk as I was seen out until 1 am, snooping around the American Hospital and other military sites, gave Mrs Baise a chance. She told Chipps what I had been doing, then wheeled the Leghorn into his office to tell the Major what *she* had found out or suspected. It was as good as a pantomime: Chipps had her tied up in bow knots asking *her* how *she*, such a nervous person, could possibly know where I walked at that hour three nights a week. Our Staff Corporal started to laugh, leaving the room in near hysterics. The Leghorn was smartly told that *not* being an established civil servant, she could (a) be transferred to the DCRE's office in Norwich, (b) get work in a canteen on one of the building sites, or (c) better still, accompany me on the tea-car driving round the lonely country roads serving the ack-ack boys, where she would be able to check on my subversive activities! That shut her trap. When Staff came back we all asked him what he was laughing at.

'Clap' Lane was the old farmery road up to what had once been Attleborough Hall, now demolished. At the end of it was a hutted camp for the builders' navvies, running parallel to the hospital roadway, which was out of bounds for the GIs. The 'Ladies' of Norwich, whose union did not allow them to work until after dark, did a brisk trade at the camp on Friday and Saturday nights. A very rough area, it was well patrolled by Red Caps and Snowdrops, the American equivalent. If the GI's were found there, they were marched straight away to the discreet green-lit treatment room behind the Red Cross First Aid room at the entrance to every US Camp or Air Force station, for what the Spanish call 'Americano Prophylactica'. I chose to work on Monday, Tuesday and Wednesday nights on the assumption that by then the navvies would have run out of cash so it would be fairly quiet passing the end of the lane.

Staff then enlightened us that the Leghorn was a *habitué* of 'Clap' Lane. He had it from the Red Cap in his billet. Her husband had been overseas for a year. A few months later she started fainting fits. Sly old Chipps sent Etienne up to Mrs Baise's office on some pretext with instructions to give the Leghorn the once over unobtrusively. All suspicions were confirmed, and she left a month later to go to mind her sister in Thetford!

Her mischief inadvertently did me a good turn: Chipps told me to take the Flea for my trips to Norwich and he would fiddle the mileage in the 412, the Army car log book. It made life much easier without the fear of missing the Passion Wagon.

When I was driving the Flea one morning going past Elveden Hall up the hill where the road runs between two high-banked walls, several Churchill tanks came thundering past me. As the last one came round the bend on the top of the hill, its track came off. There was no escape from this wobbling, evil, death-dealing monster advancing on the poor little flimsy Flea. I knew then what a rabbit felt like in a snake's cage. The track gained momentum down the hill and mercifully, as it veered to the right, the Flea responded and jumped ahead; as it wobbled back, it just tipped the rear mudguard, swinging the little car round. Had it gone over us we would have been like a piece of very dirty pastry. The tank itself had slewed across the road, blocking it completely – I think it was the only time other than among the V2s in London that I was paralysed with fear.

D-Day was now upon us, and we used to have to take our overnight cases with us when we visited camps, in case we were kept in. The sky was dark by day and noisy by night with the bombers going over for saturation raids. The south of England was more or less cordoned off, and one had to get a permit to get to the coastal resorts.

When I received a telegram saying that my grandmother was dying and I had to get to Bournemouth urgently, Chipps was wonderful and got me a permit and free rail transport.

After my return to HQ, Chipps was promoted to CRE Solihull as his special work was no longer needed. I had a few weeks' leave before officially joining the YMCA at the end of July. Sadly, poor old Chipps did not live to see the end of hostilities. He died as he would have wished, in harness. He, in his own words, 'made fast the dinghy'.

# 3

# 'MARCHING ON TO LAFFAN'S PLAIN'

The YMCA Female HQ was in Hans Place, Knightsbridge. There, the Hon. Mrs (later Dame) Joan Marsham was the Queen Bee. At my interview was Mrs Abel Smith and dear Ann Holland Martin, the nicest of all the Cavendishes. We had known each other for years. She gave me a knowing wink. Mrs Marsham asked me all sorts of quite irrelevant questions, including, 'Was I strong?' in an ambiguous way.

I replied, 'Physically, yes. If you mean capable of lifting, I can carry a hundredweight sack of oats up a ladder.'

This reply went down in the annals of the Y as *the* most peculiar answer. Ann chipped in: 'You need have no fear for her: I've seen her ploughed into the ground under a four-year-old and she's got up and finished the hunt.'

This verification of strength was beyond poor Mrs M's comprehension. 'Well, er, yes, you seem to be strong.'

I was billeted at 2 Avenue Road, St John's Wood, in one of the attics. The initial three-month training consisted of serving 'bangers', mash, two veg. and 'arters' at the all-night canteen in Euston Station, alternating with driving a tea-car round the Surrey Docks, the Old Kent Road and Wapping.

One thing they taught me was the rudiments of catering for large numbers. Before the war, we always had good cooks. Knowing how food should look when it came to table was one thing, but the mechanics of how it got there was an enigma to me. Poor Guy was once complimented by a guest on the wonderful cook his wife was. When relating this to me, Guy said: 'I didn't have the heart to disillusion him that you could not boil water without burning it!'

I was then given my HGV driving test in an empty double-decker bus by one of the London Transport Board examiners, a brave man who stood in the passenger section whilst I was alone in the cab. Used to driving horse boxes and trailers, the tail swing was no problem to me. On the day of my test it had snowed lightly and frozen. We came down Regent Street, using my gears (which, with no synchromesh in those days) were so heavy that you had to use two hands to change them. Double-declutching, I got round Eros, but as we levelled out to go down Piccadilly the bus chassied gracefully broadside on the ice down Lower Regent Street. Letting her go until she stopped opposite Jermyn Street, I drove along it, coming back to Piccadilly via St James's Street. The only comment from the examiner was that I should be a taxi driver as I knew my London. When I was a child, my Grandfather Willie used to take me to various places in London from where I would have to find my way back to Browns Hotel – how often in the blackout did I thank him for his tuition!

The V2s were at their zenith then, and I found them more scare-making at night than any bombing raid, as I lay in bed listening to the zig-zagging thrum of their engines, waiting for the cut-out – if you then heard 'kwissh' you knew it had passed you by and the 'crump' had claimed some other victims. One of the nearest ones I had heard fall was on the Bunch of Grapes in Orchard Street when I was in the Cumberland Hotel, Marble Arch. The other was in Covent Garden when I was at a performance of Sullivan's *Merrie England*: the warning went and some of the audience left for the shelters, but having seen what was brought out of those places after a direct hit, I firmly adhered to Vandy's, and Chipps's advice – when in a raid, *stay where you are*. 'Queen Elizabeth' was just hitting the top C in 'There will always be an England' when the V2 landed. She held onto the top C but her beautiful golden wig tipped drunkenly over one eye, having been dislodged by some rendering from the ceiling. Dusty but unbowed, the cast carried on and got a standing ovation from the audience that were left, notably service personnel.

Those members of the YMCA who were selected for the British Liberation Army (later the BAOR – British Army Over the Rhine) were then billeted in South Audley Street opposite Grosvenor Chapel, ironically next to a cousin's house where I had had many happy times. On the staff were two most delightful older women, one being Miss McClean, who had been housekeeper to the

26

Cavendish Bentincks at Welbeck Abbey (now a training college). Her stories of their eccentricities would fill a book – Ottoline Morrell was truly taking after her ancestor who built all the underground carriage drives. The other, whom I shall call Miss X, had been for many years before the war one of Queen Mary's personal secretaries. She knew Guy and my father's cousins well, who had been equerries, and confirmed all they had told us about the Royal Family. She also confirmed the general consensus of opinion that with 'David's' pro-German tendencies and always choosing to speak that language in his own establishment, Ernest Simpson was a plant or 'Fall Guy', well paid by the German hierarchy, to trap the Prince of Wales and thereby bring down the British Monarchy, paving the way for a takeover bid for Hitler. But as usual no one in high places would remove their Blinkers. Winston Churchill was castigated as a war-monger, much as Margaret Thatcher is now for realising that the Trades Unions are the tools of the USSR. How I wish that tape-recordings had been invented then, for both Miss McClean and Miss X were a mine of real history. I still have a tiny English/French dictionary that the former gave me.

Of the girls in that billet I was the only driver. We went to Hans Place for a farewell bunfight in November, presided over by poor Princess Mary, looking more like an undernourished old cab horse than ever. The occasion reminded me of certain things in life which had always puzzled me: for instance, why, when perfectly nice women are put into pseudo-uniform and given a little authority, do they ninety-nine times out of a hundred become overbearing, aggressive and fail to see reason about anything? No trained service officer would behave as they do. Also, why are dedicated do-gooders in the welfare world so terribly tactless and undiplomatic?

After the Royal Patron had departed, Joan Marsham gave us a 'pep talk': 'Now, you dear girls are going into a devastated country. I want you to make everything bright for our dear boys. Go out' – here, with a histrionic gesture, she raised her arm – 'into the highways and byways and gather flowers for your canteen, then get sheets from stores, cut out bright pictures from magazines of Mickey Mouse, and appliqué them onto the sheets; these make wonderful curtains and the boys love them! Organise games and competitions, but dears, above all, make your canteen bright!' Not one word as to dealing with the men's problems! She ended: 'Good luck and God bless you all. I shall be behind you and thinking of you out there

27

when my chauffeur collects me, my butler has a much-needed drink ready for me and my maid will have run my bath as I like it – but my mind will be with all of you out there!'

In our draft, with the exception of one older woman, the other four were from provincial urban backgrounds and would not have known what to do with a lady's maid if they had met one.

The regulation 'pepper and salt' grey Y uniform was nice, if well cut, but the battledress material was a pale blue-grey. It was obligatory to get one uniform from Simpsons – shirts, ties, cap and a beret. For the other uniform it was up to each individual to select a tailor. Having seen the hit-and-miss tailoring of the Simpsons uniforms on the others, I opted for the battledress there and the dress uniform to be made by our own dear old family tailor in Cork Street. He clucked and fussed over me like a hen with a duckling, cutting my coat about two inches longer than regulation, with a single vent, as this suited my peculiar figure and could then be used for hacking as well. The regulation skirt had too much of a 'gardening lady's' flare; this we straightened out. The greatcoat material looked like the homespun frieze coats which the west of Ireland farmers wear, but without the warmth or body, so I asked if I could have a 'British warm' for the coupons instead. Certainly, but it would be more expensive. Then he said he could let me have one without coupons that they had in stock, ordered on his last leave by a poor young officer who would no longer need it. Very tactfully put! It fitted me superbly and was duly tricked out with the two silver-and-blue stripes on the epaulets.

It was also obligatory that we got our shoes from a shop in Sloane Street. These were 'clumpers' with toecaps. Owing to a badly broken instep and peculiarly shaped feet, these horrors were out of the question for me, as the nice shop-assistant admitted. Having been brought up on the premise that foot comfort, whether for man or horse, is of paramount importance, I got a letter from a doctor excusing me that type of shoe. Having in the meantime gone to Hills of Knightsbridge, who had my last, I ordered two pairs of black shoes of the Monk type (the highly fashionable and very comfortable 'polite' walking or town wear of the day), with heavier soles than usual. The other obligatory things were a blue poplin dress and a school-type belted raincoat. We were also issued with a tablet of Park Davis anti-lice soap, hard, gritty and smelling abominably of sulphur and creosote.

At our send-off bunfight several of the VIPs had remarked how well-cut and nice my uniform looked (they never noticed the shoes). I felt rather a heel among the poor sheep who had gone where they were driven, taking what they were offered without demur, but like Brer Rabbit and the Tar Baby 'I lay low and said nothing'!

The next day we all assembled at Y HQ in Russell Street with our baggage. My bedroll, consisting of the famous horse blankets purchased without coupons in Newmarket and supplemented by two more from the PX, wrapped up in the groundsheet, contained my field boots, riding breeches, British warm, the khaki battledress, well-cut by Miss Compodonico of Newmarket for use in Attleborough, sheepskin jerkin, a little black dress, an evening dress and two pairs of smart shoes. The old-fashioned kitbag held the official uniform, towels, an Army Bible and prayerbook given to me by my friend George Perdue, the Rector of Snailwell, the complete works of Guy de Maupassant and *The Ingoldsby Legends*. I boldly wore the ghastly raincoat.

We were lined up for a briefing by the head of the YMCA, Adam (later Sir Adam) Scott, the men on one side of his office, the 'ladies' on the other. The four male drivers and I had a non-driving passenger each. Our tea-cars were in Bedford Square, whence we would collect them and bring them to HQ for our baggage, then proceed in convoy to Tilbury for embarkation after dark. After a brief pep talk on the aims and objects of the Y – in short, get religion into the men via their stomachs – he then turned to us 'girls', telling us that we would be working alongside Y men who were not in any way like our brothers and relations in the Guards' regiments! With the exception of the older woman and me, this did not apply, but in front of the four male drivers it was the most awful gaffe. Here let me say that Y drivers, storemen and forward-area tea-car drivers were wonderful, dedicated men, some Non-conformist Ministers, some 'conshies' or unfit for active service, with a few exceptions, but, as Scott so tactlessly pointed out, *not* out of the same stable as cavalry officers.

After tea and stale sandwiches, we had a short service led by Adam Scott, collected our tea-cars, which were loaded down to the axles with stores, were given an inventory of each load, collected our baggage and went our way in convoy to Tilbury. For my sins I was given a sprog new tea-car, not yet run in, and, as the next most experienced driver to the leader, had to bring up the rear. Everyone knows the first vehicle is only doing 15 mph whilst the last is belting it all out to keep up. The engine was as stiff as hell; it was a miracle we arrived. Then the fun started. The other three male drivers could not back onto the tank landing craft. Admittedly it was dicey, but the Rail Transport Officer did not help the poor men by bawling at them. The other women had so many bits and pieces of luggage that they kept forgetting which they had what in, taking high dives into their belongings. The leader and I duly parked the tea-cars, a small army convoy and an ambulance completed the cargo, the ramps were pulled up, and we were away.

We were battened down below like cattle. The ladies were allocated a makeshift cabin to which the four of them retired, armed with a multiplicity of pills called Quells. Someone had left hers in her luggage and wanted to get them but was soon 'sat on', and borrowed from the others. We dropped anchor in the Thames estuary where there was a slight swell. That did it; they all promptly puked. Taking myself and my half-bottle of brandy outside, I made friends with two sapper officers going back from leave and a Scots Padre who had a good bass voice and was to do with the 'Church of Scotland Huts'. To this day I do not know what a Church of Scotland Hut looks like, nor in the nine months I served overseas did I see hide or hair of one. We were joined by some of the officers of the landing craft, who had an extra NAAFI ration, so we whiled away the hours of dark singing the Sappers' song, 'Hurray for the CRE' ('You make fast, I make fast, make fast the dinghy . . . For we're marching on to Laffan's Plain . . .). One man from the Buffs contributed 'The Buffs the Buggers have gone away' to the tune of 'An Hundred Pipers'. This got the Padre going, so a merry time was had by all, despite two submarines chasing us. We nearly ended up at Le Havre instead of Ostend. One of the poor Y men was very sick, I tried to be nice to him, offering him some brandy, but he refused, being a teetotaller. The others, after Adam Scott's statements, looked on me with the greatest suspicion.

After about eighteen hours on board, we disembarked on what was left of the quay at Ostend and headed for Brussels. We were billeted in a small hotel taken over as a transit hostel for the Y. Washed and fed, we were taken to the Queen Bee who ran the Big Canteen, which was more like a Lyons Corner House. In the evening Violet McCraith, my supposed second-in-command, and I went to the Officers' Club for a drink, as the Y officially does not permit drink on its premises. There were quite a few people we knew. When we got back to our billet the other four, still more dead than alive, were full of the canteen work.

Next day we were to go to Y GHQ for our postings at noon. The four others clung to Violet and me like lost dogs. I took them round Brussels, which had not been too badly damaged, ending up with what my Grandmother 'Georgie' and her cousin 'Bertie' used to call that 'poor incontinent little boy' (the Manakin Pisse). I managed to buy some postcards of him and the nuns praying that their car might break down while passing him, which I sent to various friends. The four ladies did *not* think it was very nice. There were about a dozen women at HQ for re-posting. A very tall American Y man spoke to us and was the first person to give any inkling of the actual welfare work involved other than tea and prayers. He also reiterated Chipps about looking after yourself. In his words, by listening to others' troubles you were 'burning yourself up' and must refuel. Then Bill Laing, the great Panjandrum, spoke a lot of waffle, giving the impression as usual that neither Eisenhower, Patton or Monty could really have got on so far without *him*. While he was blathering on, to keep myself awake I looked out of the window onto a side street, to be entertained by two GI's copulating with two girls in the same doorway and a mongrel dog and bitch emulating them a few feet away. The session droned on, the girls were all allocated to various canteens, then Bill Laing, shuffling his papers, turned to Violet. 'So nice to have you with us – you're the late Sir Robert McCraith's daughter, a sister of the present Sir Robert?' How that bombast dearly loved a lord! I was so thankful I reverted to being plain Miss. Re-shuffling his papers, he called my name. Now I was beginning to sweat – would my gamble to be sent forward pay off? His opening gambit did not improve his image with me. 'I see you're Irish – are you a member of the IRA?' His facetiousness was unwarranted. I lost my temper and from then on we were at daggers drawn. I told him pretty sharply that there was no conscription in Ireland in either war and the cream of our Irish manhood had given their lives for England, and thought his joke in extremely bad taste. Dear Bob (Robbie) Roberts, my beloved 'Buffer State' and Laing's second-in-command, kicked him under the desk, and he did a sort of ungracious apology.

All eyes in the room were on me. My Irish hackles were up and

31

they were also curious about my not being posted with them. Laing then announced: 'You will go forward to a Mobile Static as Leader. Will you take Miss VM with you? Mr I. Manson will collect you at the hostel after lunch.' A Mobile Static was a canteen working in a house but moved forward with the unit to which it was attached, the Leader coming under military command of that unit. I believe it was the only such unit in the BLA.

Here I must state there were many dedicated men and women in the Y, but for me the ones who carried the show and kept it running in the BLA were Robbie Roberts, George Upton, the Forward Area Secretary under whose command I was, Don Tyler, another full-time US Y man, and dear Harry Hunt. But it was Robbie Roberts who kept the whole outfit together and smoothed out Laing's *faux pas*. When medals were dished out after peace broke out, it is to the Y's everlasting shame that Robbie did not get one. He had to wait forty years to get his CBE; he should have been knighted.

As for me, from the Y point of view, I was from the first a total dead loss.

# 4

# '240 UP' TO TESSENDERLOO

We set off for Hasselt, about forty miles from Brussels, in the early afternoon. It had been snowing fairly heavily all day but the convoy's track vehicles had made the road semi-passable give or take the odd shell-hole or mined areas taped off. The tape was difficult to see against the snow. Our courier was, I believe, called Ianson, a grand man, ex-army veteran of the 1914–18 war. His stores and HQ was at the Y in Hasselt, his job to transport the 'rookies' to their new assignments. Except for Violet, who slept and *snored* most of the way, we chattered away like magpies. Meg Aldridge, the Hasselt canteen Leader, gave us a great welcome, a hot meal, and sped us on our way to our civilian billet for the night. We ate and talked to the familiar thud of heavy artillery; the odd V2 wending its way to the UK went over.

The first hint of my troubles was when Violet kicked up hell's delight about sharing the small bedroom with me and absolutely refused to let me sleep in my bedroll on the big bed which nearly filled the room. She had a huge, very expensive, fleece-lined sleeping bag. I got what sleep I could on the floor, with her snoring loudly all night and champing her teeth. She complained unceasingly about the primitive conditions of our billet and the non-communication – the owners of the house, only spoke Flemish and a little bad French, and were not able to understand her Roedean brand of 'the pen of my aunt'. Mr Ianson listened patiently at breakfast to her moanings, but I could see he was *not* amused. While we were loading the three-ton lift with all the extras for the canteen at Tessenderloo which was to be our destination that day, she went to look round the little town, got two falls on the snow and twisted her ankle – a good start!

We knew that 27 CRASC (Command Royal Army Service Corps) the leading supply unit of the British Army, which was to be my unit until peace broke out, had got a house for the canteen and had it cleared. That was all. The CO was away, so Major Willis of the 18 Coy Pioneer Corps was to install and feed us until we got sorted out. We had to sleep in the empty house until the canteen furniture arrived from Brussels for which Mr Janson and I made out a list after we had seen the size of house etc.

Violet's first *faux pas* was sitting down to dinner in Mess with her cap on, and next day at lunch with her greatcoat as well, after which Major Willis yanked me into the orderly room and blew his top. I was to tell her how to behave in Mess. I had already done so, only to be told that she was the age and standing that would always wear a hat if asked out to lunch, and that she was *not* in the army. I had to explain this as tactfully as I could. At dinner that night, Major Willis and all the other officers appeared in caps, Sam Brownes, greatcoats, mufflers and their small arms in holsters. After grace, the Major turned to me with an evil leer, remarking: 'Your second-in-command has started such a cosy fashion in Mess, I thought we might try it.' The shot went home, she excused herself, saying she did not feel well. When out of earshot, the Major said: 'She'll feel a damn sight worse when Colonel Mumford gets back!' I found her on her camp-bed in tears. Snuffling, she told me she would not eat in that nasty common old man's Mess again with all those nasty little bank clerks. I suggested she would be hungry. 'Oh no dear,' she replied, 'you can bring it to me.' Dear had no such intention.

Colonel Mumford came back a day before he was expected, so I did not have time to do the correct thing by calling on him. He came in, cheery as a cricket, to be met by Violet in the hall, delighted to see him and bubbling over with complaints about the discomfort and the insolence of Major Willis, ending up, before he had time to open his mouth, by telling him she expected to get the OBE for her pioneering capabilities.

Colonel Mumford was a tiny little man, but when on his mettle looked like a six-footer. 'I came to call on the Leader, not to listen to your complaints. Where is [and here he *was* naughty, because we were only entitled to use the honorary rank of Captain when taken prisoner] Captain Pyne Clarke?'

Her answer nearly floored him. 'She's in the kitchen cleaning my shoes.'

This *contretemps* was retailed to me in full at a later date by both the Adjutant and the Company carpenter, who was making a counter for the canteen. The CO stalked past Violet, saluted the 'boot black' smartly, introduced himself and the Adjutant, then let fly: 'That bloody old b— out there is no use here. She'll get the OBE from me – Order of the Boot and Evacuation. She is to be off these premises in twelve hours or less. I will send a despatch to Brussels, and she can go back with the empty stores truck.'

Go back she did. She worked as a cashier in one of the Brussels canteens, living the life of Riley for six months, and then got tired and returned home. After her departure I was on my own except for one nice, delicate boy who was 'bomb happy' (shell-shocked), a Forward Area tea-car driver sent to me for a 'rest' about three months later in Kevelaer in Germany. When the first shell landed in the Jerry metal factory opposite the canteen, he fled and was found later wandering in Louvain on the Dutch border, with no idea how he got there.

'The Damsel Fair' was written by Mr Asquith, one of 'the nasty little bank clerks', on the head of Violet's departure. He was, I believe, an estate agent, a brilliant actor, and could write serious verse as easily as doggerel.

## The Damsel Fair

The shades of night were falling fast
As through Tessenderloo there passed
A van emblazoned with Triangle Red
Which straightway to 18 Company sped
And proceeded to deposit there,
Two damsels (one was dark, one fair),
Who'd come from England recently
To find a house, which, furnished decently
Would make a cosy canteen where
The tired soldiers could repair
Each evening when the work was done,
And there o'er cup of tea and bun,
Discuss the war with other chaps
Or write a letter home, perhaps.
These maidens (one was fair, one dark),
Before the van had time to park,
Invaded 18 Company's Mess
And occupied it – more or less
For the officers, all gentlemen,
Were mightily afraid of them.
The damsel who was rather dark,

35

Soon found this life was rather stark
And, creature comforts being rare,
She packed, and left the damsel fair
To face alone the toil and trouble
And left for Brussels at the double;
The damsel who was rather fair
Proceeded promptly to ensnare
All officers from miles around
Who, to their consternation, found
They'd each been cast to play a part
In giving this canteen its start.
But each gave nobly of his best
And served the damsel fair with zest,
Whilst she felt not the least remorse
At driving each one like a horse.
And so by scrounging here and there,
This go-ahead young damsel fair
Got canteen going with a swing
(Selling cups of tea, and everything),
And though all nobly did their bit,
In making this canteen a hit
I think the credit's mainly due
To the dashing damsel fair – don't you?

Tessenderloo was a small town between Hasselt and Eindhoven. Its west end had been devastated by the explosion of what was officially designated a 'Soap Powder Factory', but which had been busily making explosives even prior to the war. There were two rocket-launching pads a little way to the east of the town on the Dutch Roermond border. Passing over the town, the rockets were only gaining height, and their vibration used to shake the houses. It was common practice to wave them on over your head, whether in Mess or in the street. The children sang a jingle, half-Flemish, half-soldier-slang: 'Nix in the winkle, nothing in the shop, and the flickety bombs going over the top.'

The Ardennes line had been stabilised but the snow was still thick on the ground. The streets and '240 up' (the main military route into Germany) were deep in slush, with high drifts of snow on either side, particularly on the country lanes. There were quite a few detachments of Pioneers away from the town. Colonel Fritz Renton, an old friend and Pioneer Corps Commander, sent me up his horse that he had found on the beaches to ride out to these lads, bringing them chocolate, cigarettes and any small thing they needed. This was done after the morning opening of the canteen.

All Irish riders know that one of the occupational hazards when riding a fresh horse is the dish or bucket of dirty water chucked out of the cottage door by the lady of the house, with the same gay abandon as the Cork Shawlies, pulling the shawls round their heads, stepped out into the path of a tram, car or fast-trotting horse and trap without the slightest glance to see if anything was approaching. The Flemish ladies were no exception to their sisters in the Emerald Isle. D Day, as the horse was called, had only one failing. He would walk under a Churchill tank, or stand like a statue under shellfire, but he shied madly at 'nothing'. This day, the pail of water was too much for his stoicism. Whipping round, he slipped, landing himself upside down in the snowdrift with me underneath him. The more he struggled, the harder he packed the snow, wedging himself on his back like a shoeing frame in reverse. Fortunately, as the noisome drain at the roadside was deep, I was able to burrow my way out. As I surfaced, there were muffled sounds of a vehicle stopping, and English voices: 'You catch his tail, I'll take his ears, get the trenching shovel out . . .' Obviously our rescuers were horse-minded, and they were all concern for the 'poor chap' underneath. As usual, I had been making a few uncomplimentary remarks about the Belgian population in general. Shaking the snow off myself like a cocker spaniel coming out of a pond, I stood up as they righted poor DD. They then looked at me in awe. One of them was a Padre attached to the 'Cherry Pickers' (the 11th Hussars). My sheepskin jacket had saved me from being horribly wet, but I smelt worse than any skunk. I was told afterwards that when the Padre was relating the incident to a friend of mine, he remarked: 'She was in no real danger, the language that she used would have soon melted the snow.'

The house the canteen was in had been a Gestapo HQ where they tortured and shot members of the local Maquis. At the end of the garden was a red-brick wall with two places in it spattered by bullet holes with a significant outline in the middle of the holes. This was their execution wall: the ground underneath was caked with blood. As the Belgians were so notoriously light-fingered, I had to put all stores in the attics at the top of the house, only issuing them each morning and afternoon to my two orderlies before the local Red Cross ladies came in for counter duties in the canteen. Stock-taking one day with Roberts, my batman, something tickled his head. Putting up his hand to brush it off, he caught a handful of human hair. It was the scalp of a woman with long hair pushed up into the crossbeams of the attic. We both felt horribly sick. This was one of the ways the Gestapo branded women whom they suspected of helping POWs to escape. When she got to know me, Matilde Geigskens, head of the local Red Cross, an extraordinary-looking woman who always wore a hat, showed me the back of her head, completely bald, the actual skull exposed, a grizzly sight. She had helped several RAF pilots who were shot down to escape, a genuine person who did not ask for a handout.

Both my family and friends who had fought in the 1914–18 war always distrusted the Belgians. Now most of them disgusted me, for if they did anything for you, gentle or simple, they boldly asked for a handout. Shortly after getting to Tessenderloo, an RAF plane crashed about two miles from the town, killing the crew of four. The 'blood wagon' and rescue workers were not more than three-quarters of an hour getting to the scene; but when they did, the crew were stripped stark naked and every instrument and part of the plane that could be moved was stripped out of it, yet 'no one had been near it'. Further down the line was a 'cage' (POW camp). When our POWs had been in it, the locals stole their Red Cross parcels and now that Jerries were in it they were doing the same to them, so much so that the Camp Commandant issued orders that if caught they would be shot out of hand. Everyone said, 'Poor little Belgium – what she had suffered,' but it was the very poor who suffered, for the rich were opulently so, hopping out of bed with the Germans and into bed with the liberating forces. The medics used to say irreverently that the biggest casualties of the War were caused by Tilly lamps and Brussels leave!

One evening a very grand old local comtesse called on our CO, inviting him, his second-in-command, Adjutant and me to dinner. It was the usual long-drawn-out affair, long pauses between each course, enormous log fires blazing at either end of the big hall in which we dined, all the right wines to go with each course, beautiful silver (which like most continental silver was very dark), excellent napery and table appointments. As the feast drew to its wearisome end, she took the Colonel's hand, saying, 'Now I've given you this lovely meal and invited your paramour as well, you can do something for me. Here is a list.' She only wanted five tons of coal plus unlimited petrol, sugar and coffee.

Standing stiff as a ramrod, our CO barked: 'Gentlemen, we have been invited to a meal as a bribe, so we will take our leave after Madame La Comtesse has apologised to Captain Pyne Clarke.' The old girl turned purple with rage. He also told her that if any more of her work people were found in or near the Bulk Supply Depot (BSD) they could be shot. He put a few enquiries afoot after that, and found that both she and her husband, who was *supposed* to have disappeared, were collaborators as well as the owners of the so-called Soap Powder Factory. Just before we went forward, her house was searched and her old husband found alive and well in a sort of priests' hole, with all mod-cons.

The country graveyards in that part of Belgium had the stark coldness of the Welsh hillside ones except that photographs of the 'dear departed' were inset into the headstones. Riding by one of these little graveyards one day I saw that a burial was in progress just inside the low wall. On my return journey, the grave was filled in, the mourners departed. Two days later as I passed, six men were busily opening up the same grave. On my return, the coffin was open at the graveside, the lid badly smashed from being wrenched off, the cadaver in his best black suit was out on the ground, five of the men were literally 'frisking' him, going through *all* his pockets, the sixth had a shoe in his hand and was tearing out the lining and shaking the shoe vigorously. The man who wrote 'The Damsel Fair' came along in his 15 cwt truck. Stopping for a chat, he joined me in looking over the wall. If he is still alive he can testify to what was going on. We never found out who the cadaver was or what was the object of the exercise.

When I lived in Newmarket I had met that King of Tramps, 'The Long Man'. He was 6 foot 6 inches in height, wore an old, very high-crowned felt hat, adding to his stature, and was of very mixed European race. His worldly possessions were in a charette which he called 'Lizzy'; his wife I never saw as she had got too feeble to tramp with him and was permanently in a hospice of some kind, where he would winter as he too was feeling his age. He tramped Europe, spoke seven languages fluently, was an authority on hieroglyphics, Ancient Greek and Latin. Earning a meagre living by helping authors and clergy with translations, he wrote a book called *The Long Man*, which I was lent. The gipsy blood in me is very strong: his lifestyle appealed to me so much that I made it my business to meet him. He told me of the famous tree in the Ardennes, giving me a map and explicit instructions as to its whereabouts, adding that if I did visit it a contribution to the food cache was a 'must'.

One of the 'nasty little bank clerks', David, was an anthropologist of some note, so when the Ardennes was cleared of Jerries, I enlisted his help in getting permission from Colonel Mumford to go on a 'swan' for half a day. David visited 'Recovery' (where the smashed crates were repaired and repacked, and where there were always a few tins spare for which no room could be found) in the BSD. I took a biscuit tin of coffee, tea, chocolate and sugar from my own stores, and we set off. The snows were melting fast by then and the forest was an eerie and macabre place, with burned-out tanks with the crews still in them. One Panzer tank had its officer's body still standing in the gun turret, his head shot clean off but his powerful field glasses still on his chest, their strap round the stump that was his neck. Still unburied Allied and German dead were being uncovered by the melting snow. The fighting had smashed a lot of the landmark trees, but the map the Long Man had given me was exact, and we found it. Miraculously intact, it was as if a preservation order had been placed on that area of the forest. The tree itself was an Aladdin's cave, with every conceivable cooking utensil, spotlessly clean, hanging round it, and inside a haven of refuge with fresh branches and pine needles making a luxurious couch. That we were under observation there was no doubt, but not a twig cracked or a branch stirred. Placing our contribution in the concealed cache, David took some photos. We made tracks for our vehicle, well pleased with our 'swan'. Just before we reached the truck, my arms were quietly pinned to my sides, David's also, and a third figure materialised. No word was spoken as the camera was taken. Removing the film, the 'front man' handed back the camera and pointed to our vehicle. We were released and never saw our captors. All was done in discreet and absolute silence.

There was a wonderful atmosphere round the tree, as of a meeting of many cultures in complete harmony. I do so hope that progress has not discovered and desecrated it. Peace was there even though the thud and crash of gunfire was ever present.

★ ★ ★

The canteen at Tessenderloo was running well and the men were getting to know me. I insisted that padres of *all* denominations were welcome, and if possible that they take the Epilogue in turn each night when we closed so that no soldier felt that his religious beliefs were left out.

The whole house in Diest Strasse, however, gave me the most awful revulsive, creepy feeling, particularly when returning from the outside privy late at night. There always seemed to be a lot of people in great stress milling round the garden, unseen but very much felt. Coming back through the garden late one night, this feeling was stronger than ever when a diminutive figure loomed up in front of me. 'It's all right, Tess [I was now 'Tessie Loo' to all the officers, but I held out against the 'Loo' so was 'Tess'], it's Tiger Tim [my name for Colonel Mumford, shortened and affectionately adopted by his HQ staff to T. T.] Go back down the path, I want to talk to you.'

In the eerie darkness, with the guns for background music, he informed me that 54 BSD had pulled out of 30 Corps and was on its way to Eindhoven in Holland and I *would* be packed up and pulling out by 5 am to go forward with his HQ, *and* I *would* be open for business at 6.30 pm next evening, where he knew not, but he would find a space somewhere for me. We walked through the house assessing the 'lift' (tonnage of transport needed) and manpower required for packing. With the aid of my batman and orderly guard plus a few long-suffering Pioneer officers, the three Maxes were loaded, mobile generator, water carrier and field kitchen hitched on, and we were away by 4.30 am. Fortified by strong tea and spam sandwiches, we set out on the 240 up. In peacetime it would have taken little over an hour, less now with the motorways, but with shell-holes, unexploded mines taped off, other convoys, plus a few breakdowns, we got into the Philips factory at Eindhoven at 3 pm. In my wisdom I had packed all the furniture and heavy stores in two of the Maxes, leaving all the immediate requirements for a quick set-up in the third. This paid off, as we had only a small office from which to work. We *were* open for business as usual at 6.30 pm.

With the exception of CRASC HQ and some transport drivers, all the BSD men were new to us, a good few complaining that there were no facilities like the Brussels Ys that they were used to, which, as I have said before, were more like Lyons Corner Houses as they were in large buildings, either small hotels or restaurants. Poor lads, they got a nasty shock because their own workload was increased threefold. The Dutch civilian labourers, unlike their Belgian counterparts, were so starved and weak that they could not shift the stores, many fainting; one or two, I believe, died from exhaustion. The CO was quick to see this and gave orders that the civilian workers were to be fed on site twice a day. Some of the men tried to conceal their food to take home to their hungry children. It was remarkable the difference the good food made to the poor men. The BSD was then working twenty-four hours a day, but with civilian labour the shifts and rest periods were spaced out.

My furniture was stored in a shop next to HQ in the main street and I moved to a pastry shop next door. Taking two tea urns, boxes of those awful oblong ginger biscuits and a huge box of writing paper, bootlaces, hankies etc., out in the Padre's 15 cwt during the morning, going up to the two forward Detail Issue Depots after dinner in Mess, I would 'brew up' an urn in the shop and hold what MP's call a 'clinic' for any of the lads who had problems or wanted letters written. The canteen, if it could be called that, was working at only half-cock, since we were only marking time before going forward as soon as the roadhead was captured at Kevelaer.

I was billeted with a very rich furniture manufacturer's family, the den Dungens. Mei Frau was a typical Dutch woman, her whole life revolving around her husband and son, the latter having been concealed in the roof space all through the occupation where he had studied hard. He was exercised like a dog at night by his father, who pretended he was an imbecile and could not speak. The daughter of the house, Mies, attended De Vlierd Agricultural College, doing a government-sponsored course for the help of the very poor and illiterate southern Dutch farmers. The curriculum included maternity, baby care and horticulture as well as agriculture, animal husbandry, dairy and domestic work. The girls were then sent to 'live in' with these families for, I believe, an eighteen-month period to instruct both husband and wife in the management of house and farm. Mies was a grand girl: in my spare time she took me to some of these awful farms. I had never realised that the Dutch could be so slovenly, but I noticed that it was on the Flemish Belgian border that most of these were, the further north one went the cleaner and more meticulous the standard of living becoming.

Mies took me to a riding school – with one horse! He was a delightful Arab stallion, whose owner had saved him by putting his forelegs in plaster of Paris, which made him sore and lame – he never grew hair on them again. He was recovering when I met him, and the owner, who had been badly beaten up by the SS, could not ride him, so was delighted when I offered to exercise him. I have always had a great affinity and get on well with stallions, and he was no exception. We pottered round what is known as the 'environs' of Eindhoven and the lake round which there was a nice circular ride just about right for him and for the time I had free. The last time I rode him, he saved both our lives. Monty was really laying down the heavy stuff and the noise was terrific. Coming home to the stable I took a short cut, a very lovely path through the wood. Pasha knew it well. Suddenly he stopped, and nothing would induce him to go on. Whipping round, he bolted for about half a mile. As he stopped, a shell hit the path exactly where we would have been had we gone on. He settled down walking home quite calmly. His owner, who knew where we would have been when the explosion occurred, was sure he would never see his little horse again. In 1950 I went back to the BAOR and saw Pasha – he remembered me. He was then a pensioner and only used as a sire.

The nuns in Eindhoven made me laugh, whizzing about on bicycles at a rate of knots, their habits tucked up to their knees – how shocked their Irish sisters would have been!

Two other things stick in my mind about Eindhoven. First, I acquired 'transport', i.e. a paratrooper's bike known as the 'flying machine'. It was all in sections, the saddle was sharp compared with a Gillette blade, the tyres were flat and the fork slightly twisted, so you had to manoeuvre it like a motorbike and sidecar combination. The steering was possible if you leant into the sidecar, and so it was with the 'flying machine', let it go its own way to the left and you were in business. It did its duty nobly for the ten days I was in Eindhoven, but sadly, while I was busily waving to a convoy of the 51st, I rode it into a shell-hole where it literally disintegrated beneath me. It gave the poor lads going up to be butchered a jolly good laugh.

On the CO's orders I had to be collected from the billet for dinner after dark. Mei Frau insisted on giving me an enormous and beautifully done omelette, as she thought army food was no good. If there is one thing I loathe, it is a properly done frothy omelette. All was well as long as Frank Conway-Upton, the Adjutant, came for me – he loved them! Then after a chance remark I made about seeing oysters so cheap in a shop, she changed to giving me a dozen delicious oysters before going to Mess, and I would save a few for Frank. When he was away, one of the Lieutenants who came for me found me polishing off the oysters and could not keep his trap shut when we got back to Mess. The CO was also away, and the second-in-command, Dick Lewis, nearly did his nut: shellfish were out of bounds for the troops for health reasons. He sent for the Mess Orderly and a bottle of castor oil, and I was publicly dosed with a dessertspoonful of it in the Anteroom. I told him the cure was worse than the disease I was likely to get from them. How Frank and T. T. laughed when they came back and heard the story!

The REME boys took pity on my lack of transport after the demise of the 'flying machine', and presented me with 'the Mongrel': this was a large and fearsome motor bicycle made up of bits and pieces: its kick-start was too heavy for me, so I sat on it, Roberts pushed. I held it on the clutch while he jumped up behind, and we were away. Any of the lads who knew me used to make great play of jumping into the ditch, or shinning up a tree or lamp-post for safety as I passed. It all added light relief to my grizzly life-style.

A white demon with a halo round his head, one eye closed, arms outstretched, thumbs up, painted on a foot-square of blackboard with the legend 'The Old One-Two' stencilled round him, hung behind the CO's chair in his office. Above, the other legend, 'Miracles are easy, the impossible takes a little longer.'

In army parlance, the Old One-Two was the clip of your hand or gloves either side of the face that you gave a prisoner to 'straighten him up like'. It had become a favourite 'buzz' word of T. T.'s. Some wag had done the caricature. This became the special 27 CRASC sign, painted on all the HQ staff cars. At Frank's birthday party in Eindhoven, I was honoured by being made a fully paid up (with my NAAFI rations) member of the Old One-Two. By then I had become part of the 'family' with all HQ staff except for one man. Even when he was first introduced to me by the CO, he refused to either salute or speak to me. His hatred of me from the first was so intense that everyone could feel it, like the heat blast from a furnace door. If he wanted me to pass him something at table, he asked the man next to me if 'Madam Know All' would be so kind as to permit him to have the whatever-it-was. I treated it as a joke, taking it whence it came, but it was no joking matter with

the others. When the small ceremony of being made a member of
the Old One-Two took place, this man flew in the most awful rage
and stormed out of the Anteroom. Nothing anyone could do, even a
dressing-down from the CO, would make him address me directly
or salute me. Although very good at his job, the men loathed him
even before I ever appeared. He raged like a demon when T. T.
ordered 'The Old One-Two' to be painted on the Mongrel's front
mudguard.

After peace broke out, we had a farewell party for T. T. Unknown
to me, they had sent Roberts for my horse, Erna, who was brought
into the Mess and made an honorary member of the Old One-Two.
T. T. then presented me with the original Old One-Two and was
about to hand me the strip of timber with the 'Miracle Legend' on
it when this man seized it, smashing it in pieces over his knee. It
was a highly unpleasant episode at such a jolly party. No one ever
knew why he hated me so much, because his reputation for women
in general was very far from savoury. In private life he had been an
executive in a shipping company, and good at his job. Today the
Old One-Two hangs in my kitchen, having escaped being destroyed
with all my other notes and papers, by being at the bottom of a tack
chest. If by another miracle any other members of the Old One-
Two are alive and read this, it will make them smile, as we all knew
it was a naughty cartoon of T. T.

At this time I had my personal worries: Vandy had come through
the Monte Cassino campaign all in one piece, but was badly
wounded in the fighting round Falaise. We missed each other all the
time; he was sent home just as I was sent out. As usual, he made
light of it, but was now back in hospital again to have what he
described as 'some of Jerry's ironmongery' removed. It was not
until I got home that I discovered his left side had been raked by
shrapnel. He swore all our friends to secrecy about the extent of his
wounds. In addition, a doctor cousin had written telling me that
Father was under observation and losing weight. They could find
nothing but it was not a good omen.

As I was coming in from a particularly nasty experience of seeing
two sappers killed by snipers as they were repairing lines, the CO
sent for me before I got to my billet. On his desk I saw an open
letter in the Lady Mother's handwriting, and immediately feared
the worst. 'Is it my Father?'

T. T. was stern but kind: 'No, but this letter is very disturbing.' I was shocked as well by the illiterate way that my mother, a Colonel's daughter, had addressed the envelope to 'Officer in charge', etc.

The rough outline was an appeal to the CO to send me home or give her *full* details of where I was and what I was doing, because – and here was the cruel part – I had given them a lot of worry in the past by running away with a most undesirable man, going through, she *believed*, a form of marriage with him, but she was thankful to say he had been killed early in the war, and now my family were highly embarrassed as everyone knew the type of girl who did welfare work. She also named a local man, Major X, who wrote every week to *his* mother, who knew *exactly* where he was and *what* he was doing, whereas all they got from me was a jumble of letters and numbers as an address, so were unable to tell anyone where I was.

T. T. was very upset for me, so I had to tell him the truth. 'That,' he said, 'explains the two wedding-rings and the other engagement ring. I did not know Guy, but I heard of him, so you have nothing to be ashamed of.'

'No, certainly not.'

'But now, as to Major X, do you know this man?'

'Yes, all my life. Where is he?'

'In a cushy job in the Caribbean, plus wife and children, and never heard a shot fired in anger. What am I to do about this letter? She is obviously out to make trouble.'

I told him to have it copied and send it back with a note to my father, asking him to restrain my mother from writing such scurrilous letters. I would enclose both in a letter to my uncle so that she would not open it as she did all letters at home. T. T.'s face was a study: 'She opens all letters?'

'Yes.'

He was a real trooper and kept my secret, never giving me any quarter because of the man I had been married to, as would the Y hierarchy or many a lesser man. What T. T. said to my father I knew not, but he was inordinately proud of me, for years later he introduced me as 'my daughter; she was the most forward civilian woman in BLA', adding with his lovely sense of humour, 'We all knew she was always a "forward hussy".' T. T. also took great trouble to find out the extent of Vandy's wounds and asked if I would like to go home if they were very bad. The MO's report to him was favourable, and Vandy told me to stick where I was, as he would be fighting fit by the time my year's contract was up.

# 5

# BLA INTO GERMANY

As usual, we left Eindhoven as thieves in the night, but I had gone forward the day before to inspect two possible premises in Kevelaer. It was sad going up the Venlo Road to see the fresh graves; many of them had been our friends. The Guards Armoured Division took a hell of a punishing there. It was all so unnecessary, and for that wretched little Montgomery's childish ego. If he had been a bigger man in character, he would have cooperated with General Patton and closed the Falaise Gap, thereby ending the war six months earlier. Now his ego was at it again, and he wanted to be the first to cross the Rhine. It was dreadful to see the convoys going up, men clinging like flies on tanks and tank transporters or packed like sardines in lorries. Monty was throwing human life away as surely as the Russians brought up wave on wave of troops, thinking to crush the enemy by weight of numbers.

I chose the most 'desirable' residence in Kevelaer for the canteen, just beside the BSD, a beer garden with three big rooms, a kitchen and stove. One side of the stairs was still usable to get to the bedrooms and the back of the landing still had its roof intact. The two orderlies slept there. The 'master bedroom'-cum-office had no glass in its windows, which looked onto the main Strasse (240 up) and one corner had a bit of roof intact. With my groundsheet over my bed, I was snug as a bug in a rug. There was no glass in any of the rest of the windows, so the downstairs windows had to be boarded up. At the back of the kitchen was a large garage, its outside doors locked, the only entrance via the kitchen, in which were haphazardly stacked every conceivable mine from bazookas to the dreaded Schu mine. These delectable items used to be brought in through the kitchen as the roads and fields were cleared of them.

In front of this desirable residence was what was left of a large metal factory where German helmets, water-bottles and other light metal objects were made. Jerry's range-finder had his elevation too high, so that the shells presumably intended for the BSD fell into the field beyond the factory, the occasional 'short one' landing in the metal debris making a delightful clatter.

What must have been the beer garden cellar was a single-storey annexe, barred windows abutting onto the main building. This made a wonderful store, as its tiled roof was virtually intact. The dust and filth was knee-deep all round us, but we kept the kitchen and canteen area reasonably clean by using the old Irish method of tea-leafing the floor. Poor Mrs Marsham's Mickey Mouse curtains were conspicuous by their absence! One smaller room I furnished with a few 'liberated' – not looted – easy chairs in which, if they had time, the lads could read and write. The mobile generators were running all the morning and evening sessions, so we had light and heat and the radio. Water from the carrier was brought into the kitchen by hosepipe, and the field kitchen boiler sat next to the window with its smoke-stack protruding out into the street. So, all in all, we had all mod. cons. except labour.

Roberts, my batman, was a grand chap; Thompson, my other orderly, was a good plain cook, slightly bomb-happy, excellent in stores and the kitchen, but went to pieces if faced with an officer above the rank of Captain. In his own Yorkshire words, they made him 'reet frickled', and any senior officers who came to inspect us never got their messages correctly delivered if poor Thompson was on duty.

We had with HQ a rare bird in the army, an analyst, one Major Hopkins. He travelled with his own laboratory, analysing all captured stores before their issue to the troops. He was a great sport, and when the NAAFI rations ran out he usd to make a very creditable hooch.

After the morning canteen rush was over, T. T., the 'Old Adj.', i.e. Frank Upton, Major Edwards, the BSD Commander, and I used to repair to 'Hoppy's' office for what we called teast-and-toe (tea and toast), after which he doled us out a libation to keep our spirits up. This became an eleven o'clock ritual. One morning, General M. C. Dempsey, our own Brigadier 'Pat' Esse and Colonel Wheatly of 35 Pioneer Group came to see me. Thompson was on duty: at the sight of so much 'brass' he got 'proper frickled', and when asked where I was, blurted out: 'She's in Major Hopkins's lavatory with Colonel Mumford. They go there every day at this time.' Ever after, poor Hoppy's office was known as the WC.

By now my friends at home had been organised to send weekly bundles of the English daily and Sunday papers. Millicent and Cousin Jack sent the *Irish Times* and *Field*, which were all so avidly read that the print was literally read off them.

At this stage of the war the terrific push for Germany was on. There was very heavy fighting about ten kilometres up the road between Zanten and Goch, and Kleeve in the south, and a big thrust by, I believe, the Canadians, at Geldern. We had a detachment of the Canadian Foresters about three kilometres away. With us also was 121 Field Bakery, working full blast under canvas making lovely white bread such as we had not seen in the UK for years. Their camp was almost two kilometres up the road, since field bakers usually pitched their tents on a farm through which flowed a clean stream. Further up under fire was 18 FDS (Field Dressing Station), staffed by Medical Officers of the Mountain Division, attached to the 51st Division. The stores came to the roadhead railway station or by lorry to the BSD in one continuous stream day and night. The working hours of the men, mostly Pioneers, were from when reveille was blown at 4 am to 'sundown' at 2 am, when they marched back to billets for a shave and dinner. So hours worked were 22 per day, less a canteen break in shifts of 20 minutes am and pm. They crawled in for their mug of tea and ginger biscuit, their Sten guns on the tables beside them, and most of them only took a few sips of tea and fell asleep, sprawled across the tables. An NCO would come in to roust them out and the next batch would come in. They worked like this for about six weeks, and when things really began to hot up, the RASC (Royal Army Service Corps) officers took off their jackets and worked like anyone else to move the stores.

On one morning's break, with most of the poor chaps asleep with their heads literally in their tea mugs, an officious American Y man walked in, bellowed to see the Leader, then proceeded to tear strips off me, saying that the canteen was a disgrace: I should have got windows in, and had a games room for the men – Mickey Mice all over again – and that anyway I had no right to be there as Montgomery's orders were that no women should be up near the front. I said nothing, but took his name. When he was at boiling point, Jerry took a hand in the proceedings, dropping two short ones into the metal factory. I never saw anyone go greener or disappear under a trestle table quicker. What a laugh it gave our poor tired lads. I sent a signal to George Upton, our Forward Area Secretary, who came out of the line to comfort me, telling me that the gent, who was always a troublemaker, was on his way back to base, returned without thanks.

The proudest memory I have of my war service was the note in George Upton's handwriting at the foot of the circular to all Forward Y Leaders dated 9 May 1945.


Miss O. J. Pyne Clarke                              Forward Area Office
27 Supply Unit
RASC
BLA                                          9th May 1945

Dear Paddy:-

While by the side of the road yesterday between two of our centres in Germany, listening to Mr Churchill's speech, I determined to drop a brief note of appreciation to each of our Forward Area people.

Personally, as Forward Area Secretary, and on behalf of the YMCA in the BLA I want to express my appreciation of the fine work you have done in helping the British soldier, through our service, to the close of the European conflict. I am sure you have received your thanks from him in many ways, many times during the past months, so that anything I say is in reality superfluous.

At this moment (May 9th) there is some confusion and uncertainty as to just what each of us will be asked to do in the weeks and months that lie ahead. While I have no information, I feel certain that you will be needed just as long as you yourself feel the need. I trust that you will make every plan to stay on in this service especially at this most critical time.

With every good wish;

Very truly yours,
George Upton


The letter was marked 'Censored – George Upton' and his hand-written note read: 'Sometimes I get cold chills when I think of you up there all alone. We do appreciate the fine spirit in which you do your work. Good luck. George Upton.'

*When* you crawled into your camp bed about 1 am, sleep overtook you to the sound of track vehicles on the cobbles going up to the line, the peculiar sound of the boxes being loaded and unloaded – the boys got a sort of slow clap rhythm into it – slap slap – slap – slap, then the lifts pulling in – or re-loaded out, the Maxes and Scammells making their own contribution to the orchestra. From my tiny couch I could see the star shells and tracer bullets illuminating the night sky.

There must have been a very queer streak in me: from the time I got overseas, all fears of bombs left me, and a kind of elation, as when out hunting, took hold. Also, the wrecked houses and devastated towns and cities did not have the same effect on me that they seemed to have on other people: to me it was all *déjà vu.* The smell of death, charred timber, smouldering ruins, and that peculiar acrid smell that goes with such events, were what I had lived with as a small child, having seen Cork city burning and many of our friends' houses and Royal Irish Constabulary barracks turned into burnt-out shells. The complete devastation of my own and Mummy's house had shaken me, though, since before it had always been someone else's house: and here it was again, someone else's houses and towns.

On our way forward I had stopped my convoy several times to dispatch very badly wounded animals – one horse and three cows. A fine-looking herd of Holstein cows were lying down looking very normal, but quite dead, except for a big bull threshing around unable to get up, his back shattered, one poor cow bellowing piteously with her udder shot off, and another trying to calve with all her legs shattered and one blown off.

Before I had left Attleborough, Chipps had given me a very nice light service revolver which he had had in the 1914–18 war, plus a good supply of ammo for it, and a shoulder holster. He warned me that it was strictly against the rules of the Geneva Convention for a non-combatant to carry arms, but said I should always carry a gun, letting no one see it. I was glad to have it to put these poor animals out of their misery. Rather than show my hand, I had tried to get the boys to shoot them, but they could not do it.

My last knackering job was to shoot a horse. We saw a beastly old farmer beating the skeleton of a horse with an iron bar, trying to make him pull alone one of those cumbersome tipping German ploughs usually pulled by a team of three. The horse was lurching and stumbling, and when we got to him we saw that his feet were in ribbons and bleeding, his breast raw and bleeding from deep galls, and where the old brute had been hitting him, one hip bone had split the poor tight skin. I ordered my 'men' to prod the old lad a few times with their bayonets, not too gently, while I untackled the horse (who was a thoroughbred stallion) and shot him. I then lashed the old chap to the plough, leaving him trussed up like a Christmas turkey in a slight flurry of snow. In his whinings and pleas for mercy he told us his own working horses had been taken by the retreating German transport; this poor animal was left in their place. This was true, for in their mad flight out of Holland for home they had used horse and mule transport, taking fresh animals from the farms or studs *en route* to replace the worn-out ones. A great many of these poor transports had to be shot when captured as they were in such a pitiable condition.

My prowess as a 'knacker man' got around. The day after my arrival at Kevelaer, Captain George Denis of 121 Field Bakery arrived to request my services as a 'slaughter man': a shell had ripped through the long barn-like building which housed all the farm stock, starting with pigs, calves, cows and the horses next to the dwelling house. It was a typical farmhouse of that area, very well planned – you came out of the kitchen into your barn, all under cover. The shell had spent itself at the wall and door leading to the kitchen. George was a terrific character, and we became great friends: for all his toughness, he wanted the job done with the least suffering to the animals. At that time I did not tell him what I carried under my armpit. In the Field Bakery tents, pitched five hundred yards from the farm, everything neat, clean and working full blast, the scene was a contrast to the horrific one in the barn, where there were animals and bits of animals all over the place.

With two Lugers, I worked my way up to the horse section. The farmer kept one of the German subsidised mares and a stallion. The latter, a good-looking Hanoverian, was walking round the rubble in his box with his entrails trailing. The old farmer was wringing his hands and crying. None of the soldiers, nor George, would go near the horse, who was very naturally in a state of panic, so by threats that I would shoot *him*, I got the farmer to catch him and hold him still while I shot him. Next to him was a Pomeranian: no injuries visible, but in a great state of shock and a touch of pneumonia from blast. In the end box nearest the house was a lovely two-year-old filly. She had a ghastly looking wound in her neck which was smothered in congealed blood, and a clean slice like a soup-plate off one hind-quarter. Her eye was bright, with no sign of shock – and I fell. By this time our CO had arrived on the scene. He was an innocent city man, who had never seen a bad hunting or racing cut. Addressing him for the first and only time as 'Sir', which rather threw him, I asked, 'Could I have the filly if I can cure her?'

Certain in his own mind she would not last two days, and sickened by what he had seen a woman doing, he weakly said, 'Yes, but you must be entirely responsible for her transport, and she must not interfere with your duties.'

I went to work with the Master Baker's cut-throat razor, a large bowl of permanganate of potash and a bottle of iodine, all the disinfectants the bakery could muster, cleaning off the ragged edges. I explored the hole, opened it up, got the shrapnel out, plugged the wound with bandages, ordering the filly to be turned out. Tetanus was my real worry.

The bakery boys were devoted to her, and fed her out of a 'prooving' trough as she could not stretch her head down. After two days I forbade this as I wanted her to work her neck muscles. Every morning I was at the bakery at 7 am to dress the wound and back again at 5 pm before the evening session at the canteen started. I sent George up to 18 FDS to get a shot of anti-tetanus. The Second-in-Command, a tough Scot of the Mountain Division, in civilian life a country GP from Rosshire, cooperated, coming down in his meagre off-duty time to administer the shot himself. He asked George if he could meet the filly's owner, for in his own words, 'that Lassie knows her anatomy and what she was doing'. Next day he came to the canteen with dressings and antiseptic powder for her. (Through him I also saw what medicine could do in the treatment of what used to be called 'shell-shock', now designated 'bomb happy'.)

'Erna von Kevelaer', for that was the filly's registered name, became the star attraction and mascot of the men. She added a bit of light relief, but we had one fear, that Monty would get wind of her, thereby finding me. Everyone knew he was out for my blood – I had even passed him when riding the 'Mongrel' and felt like sticking my tongue out at the nasty little beast. I was one of the best-kept open secrets in BLA, but the 'boys' were fiercely loyal to their Y leader and Erna – though she ranked first.

One evening when I had dressed Erna's wound and was having a mug of tea well laced with a drop of 'How's your granny', some lovely crusty white bread and butter, chatting to George, the sentry came in a flurry – 'Captain Poston to see you!' Poor John Poston was Monty's ADC, tale-bearer and general factotum, always looking round for something nice for his chief, who amongst his other nasty traits was inordinately fond of his belly. Without ceremony, George grabbed me, flinging me down between his bed and the canvas of the tent, dumping his bedroll and coat on top of me. As John came in, George spotted lipstick on my mug: a non-drinker, he grabbed my mug and swigged its contents down in one gulp, calling his orderly to get clean mugs and more tea for Captain Poston. John parked himself on the camp bed – if I had had a pin I could have stuck it in his backside. He discoursed with George on every subject, casually mentioning that he had seen a Y sign down the road, and asking who was the Leader. Was it a woman?'

'YMCA?' said the bland George. 'Is there, by God? Well, I wouldn't know anything about Christian young men! Now, if you had told me it was a YWCA, I might have a bit more interest in the female sector.'

John grunted – he had no sense of humour – 'There's supposed to be a woman somewhere here. It's my job to find her and get her sent back.'

'Well,' said George, 'you must know my reputation for women by now – if there was one about, I'd have bloody well found her!'

Stuffed with tea and crispy bread, armed with a supply of French bread rolls for his 'chief', poor John departed none the wiser as to whom he had literally been sitting on. The poor chap was killed just before the end of hostilities. He was known to all the sporting fraternity as 'Monty's ferret'.

In my capacity as YMCA Leader, I was the recipient of many confidences, not only from OR's and NCOs but from commissioned ranks as well. My own private dislike of Monty for his mean pettiness and the trouble he got innocent men into was reiterated in many of these confidences from men of much greater stature not only physically but in character. He resented anyone getting praise, required *all* the limelight for himself, going to great lengths, if a bereaved widow or parent wrote to him (which many of them did), in seeing that the Press published his reply in full as well as the letters of the bereaved ones. To be fair, he *had* to build his image to carry the men with him in the tough assignments of his campaign, but, brilliant strategist though he was, he spoilt it all by his smallness of mind. Had Alex, Harding or Dempsey been in on the Falaise Gap when Patton and Eisenhower had the bulk of the German forces in a trap, they would have been men enough to give the US forces their support, throwing everything we had in to close the gap, encircling the German forces. Monty was piqued at Eisenhower getting Supreme Command, and, like a naughty child, refused to play. He also gave Press photographers hell because his – in his own opinion – delightful profile *had* to be taken at a certain angle, showing off his two cap badges. All this PR stuff could have been done in a much nicer way without throwing tantrums.

He was a wonderful General, but his warped nature made him, as a man, despicable. One very senior officer who had suffered his sneering gibes all the way from North Africa, was a very fine character, loyal to the regiment. Having unburdened his hurt to me, he ended by saying, 'I suppose we can't blame him, coming from that background. If he was a horse, you would not touch him on his breeding.' It summed the whole thing up very neatly. Monty suffered from a North of Ireland Methodist heredity, coupled with a driving, dominant mother. Had he been a civilian in his native land, the very apt Irish word for him could have been a 'Slibhin' – a word which conveys a whole descriptive sentence in one word – 'a sly, small-minded person who shows off'. But he did win the war for us.

The foregoing may seem a very odd criticism from a non-combatant, but I had known Monty in peacetime, and in any case, the on-looker sees most of the game and hears most of the asides.

George Denis had a great little man as his driver, known to all and sundry as 'The Brig', his small stature, double squint, cauli-flower remaining ear – the other left somewhere in a dockyard brawl – all accentuating his garden gnome appearance. He was an excellent driver, always keeping his engine tuned for a quick 'get-away', as well as top rated in his 'chosen calling', 'cracksman' – no lock or property, except Army stuff, was hallowed to him. All you had to do was mention casually that the canteen could do with a few this or that and that you had seen such and such in a house – not directly, mind you, but in course of conversation with George in the Brig's presence – and surprise, surprise, next morning the desired article would have materialised either in the kitchen or hall of the canteen.

We were now getting quite 'classy' with two sofas, some armchairs, a piano, a blackboard and easel and a small snooker table – not very steady, but complete.

Whilst on one of my sorties to pinpoint these requirements, I got what was to me a treasure, a pearl beyond price: in a kindergarten cupboard, whilst looking for chalk, I found an abacus. I did not think such trivia would interest the Brig, and it was too awkward to carry on the Mongrel, so I stuffed it up the back of my battledress and tightened the belt. One of my chief nightmares was the nightly 'cash-up'. Always dyslectic where figures were concerned, the different currencies added to my frustration. Padre Owen, now Prebendary Noah Owen, was a brick but could not come for the cash-up every night. It had not been too bad in Tessenderloo, with only French and Belgian francs for conversion, but now we had guilders and Deutschmarks to add to the other two. So the abacus was a computer to end all computers, and I still hold them more simple and reliable than those modern contraptions.

The next bit of equipment the canteen required was a good gramophone, records and needles. There was a music shop, but unfortunately it adjoined the First Aid and MP posts. Town Majors had not reared their ugly heads yet, looting was strictly forbidden, and you had to sign for anything you took, name, rank and number. Taking a leaf out of a cunning NCO's book, I always signed with a great flourish: 'Captain Tookit, 1st Battalion. Welfare Brigade, BLA.' I bet when this came up to the Town Major for barrack damages there were a few grins and well-scratched heads.

The siting of the music shop posed a problem for the Brig, so armed with him and Roberts, we took the position in a daylight raid, walking out boldly with gramophone, records and needles, all legally signed for! Then the Brig informed me that a big field of daffodils were in bloom at the back of the station, so in my 'spare time' we sallied forth to the highways and byeways to pick armfuls of them for the canteen, and for him to take a load to the Head Unit of a field hospital that was a little way in our rear. Picking away merrily – really very stupidly as we could have trodden on a mine (it was so near the town and the wrecked buildings there was the ever-present smell of acrid burning and death) – I slipped. Putting out a hand to save myself, I plunged it very nearly elbow deep into an extremely dead German's stomach. Never at a loss, the Brig cleaned up my arm with his beret, remarking that 'the watch on his wrist would "do" Roberts' and that he expected I could use the field glasses. 'True,' I said.

'Don't worry about me, Ma'am. I've got plenty of them things'. True also! Still smelling horribly, we found a tap at the railway station where again the Brig attended to my cleaning, this time with an oily lump of cotton waste. We duly reported the body to the Casualty Post and went our way, the Brig down to the hospital, remarking that if he saw anything on the way that might help the canteen, he would see what he could do about it, and I to what was grandly called my mobile baths, i.e. A split jerrycan which, with a leg in each side and a tin mug, made a good imitation of a shower.

The Mobile Baths proper were one of the blessings of the war, helping to stamp out lice and typhus. Never situated too far behind the lines, they supplied the men with a complete issue of clean clothes and a shower. The Government in their wisdom learned a lesson from the bad communications and transport of the 1914–18 war, and put in charge of supplies men like the Salmons of Joe Lyons, Sainsburys and managerial staff of big firms, preferably dealing with the same commodities as they had in civilian life. I believe I am right in saying that though the DID's issued hard-tack rations to the Forward Areas, it was on extremely rare occasions that these were used other than the 'tin of fags' being extracted.

My oblong block of hard-tack rations, approximately 28 lbs, went with me all the way up, and it was only when peace broke out that I gave the biscuits (iron hard) to refugees. I still have the little brown painted tin with the green lettering bearing the legend 'Boiled Sweets, 5 oz net. D. LTD. packed 2/43' – it is now a button box.

Labour to run the canteen was the most urgent problem. No civilians could be employed, and with close on five hundred men going through the canteen morning and evening, it was hectic. The CO of the nearby detachment of the Canadian Forestry Brigade came to ask if his men would be allowed in the canteen. Seeing the urgency of the situation, he organised a roster of his officers. Jackets off, sleeves rolled up, they worked like lumberjacks. They were quick to pick things up like carrying a multiplicity of mugs, either full or empty, a necessity, since there was no room for trays either in the floor space or getting through the tight-packed queues waiting to be served. They were the greatest help in our midday opening for the convoys who had so little time.

Two amusing events occurred at these sessions. Two Y men came into the canteen bristling with revolvers (General Patton had nothing on them, except that his had pearl handles). They demanded a case of cigarettes, a huge tin of coffee and one dozen boxes of chocolates to take up to the line. Something about them did not ring true. We were serving the Black Watch, who were going up, and the pace was hectic. I told them they would have to wait until the men were served. They started to give lip about the slow service and I got back at them that they were in no position to criticise anyone as they were blatantly contravening the Geneva Convention by being armed, which was *not* permitted by the Y. One, with his hand on his gun, told me to get the stores PDQ. Before they knew what was happening, a really brawny Scots NCO had a half-nelson on each of them. The Canadian officer who was clearing mugs whipped their guns off them and they were frog-marched into the hall. The Canadian driver was sent for a Red Cap, who on arrival bundled them into his jeep. Their American-style jeep had on it a Y and a triangle of sorts, but, when taken down to the security post, in the back was discovered an arsenal with every conceivable small arm both British and German and enough watches, field glasses and various jewellery items stripped from the dead to set up a well-founded jeweller's shop. They were GI deserters who were running a black-market racket in Belgium, the Y uniform and triangle on the jeep having let them through the checkpoints. What became of them when handed over to the tender mercies of their US brethren I know not.

T. T. knew nothing of my Canadian 'staff', who ranged from a Brigadier to a senior NCO. On this occasion we had a large number of the 51st going up, and were working forced draft, Thompson brewing tea as fast as the water was boiled, a shuttle system of urns, the Brigadier in shirt-sleeves clearing tables, a damp teacloth on his arm as a mop. He met T. T., who asked for me.

'She's far too busy to see anyone,' was the reply. 'Here, be a kind fellow and take these into the kitchen while I collect more.' Flummoxed, T. T. meekly grabbed the mugs, to find three more strange shirt-sleeved men hock deep washing up, shuttling mugs to the serving area.

'We'll call her if you like to wait, or better still, take your jacket off and give us a hand.' Shaken, but unbowed, he looked at the jackets on the back of the chairs, a Brigadier, a half-Colonel and two crowns. Nobly he took off his own, and plunged into the *mêlée* to collect mugs. The first I knew of his presence was a shout going up: 'Och away Sauchiehall Street! What did you do, Sir, to get put on cookhouse fatigues?' Some of the men were from his old 51st Transport Unit in Italy and had recognised him – for ten minutes there was pandemonium, handshakes and reminiscences. He was one of the most popular officers I had known, strict but just, in soldiers' lingo he was 'a gentleman, and you could talk to him'. If you were ever told that about an officer, you could be sure he was 100 per cent plus.

In ten minutes the NCO had them all on their way to the slaughter and peace reigned in the canteen. That was the awful, sad thing with those jolly, laughing, leg-pulling lads – you wondered how many of them would be alive that evening.

Chipps Woodley had done a good job tutoring me. Not only did he warn me always to have a reserve of stores, equipment or my own strength up my sleeve, but also to make it my business to find out what the officers with whom I would work had been in civilian life. Solicitors, estate agents, bankers and stockbrokers – in that order of priority – should be courted men because I would be asked many questions on their subjects. In his own words: 'Let the sky pilots do their own jobs; but on the technical things you will need to be on firm and correct ground.'

The real welfare work of my job came after the canteen closed. The men came to my office-cum-bedroom in a steady stream, some with very real and tragic problems, some financial, housing, or just to have a sympathetic ear to talk about the Missus, the kids, their Mums, or show you their photographs – all very important to them. The officers I enlisted for advice included a couple of country solicitors and Colonel J. Wheatley (a cousin of Denis of that ilk), who had been a District Commissioner in, I believe, the Gold Coast and was a Prison Governor when war broke out. There were also three estate agents and a few stockbrokers and bankers. I enticed them all to my cocoa sessions after the canteen closed and they sat on anything they could find round a smelly Valour oil stove at the far end of my room, imbibing mugs of strong, sweet Carnation-milk made cocoa known locally as a 'Roberts special' – he made the best cocoa you ever drank. Their help was invaluable to me and to the men. Also they loved to relax and yarn to each other about their work and homes, but Colonel Wheatley was the Seanchai (story teller) of them all. He was also a born actor, and his imitations of eminent and learned judges' eccentricities had to be seen to be believed.

George Denis was another very good raconteur. He was born in India to a service family and, like his famous ancestor, Captain Quinn of the Guards, he was 'wild'. He used to disguise himself as a native, getting into all the feasts with his father's bearer's son. (Captain Quinn's most notorious escapade was the building of Baldoyle racecourse outside Dublin. Finding himself nearly a furlong short on the mile course, he ignored such a trifle until some trainers began to query their horses' times.) How I wish I had had the time or gumption to write their stories down.

I made all these poor chaps sit down at the far end of the room in the shadow from my Tilly lamp with their backs to the door so that the 'supplicants' coming to the 'confessional' would not see who they were, and nine times out of ten never even noticed there was anyone else in the room. Once they nearly let me down. A 'Lance Jack' (Lance Corporal) came in in a great state about his wife and what she was up to with the GI's. After listening to a long spiel about the wickedness of her family and all belonging to her, I eventually asked him why, if he knew all that about her, did he marry her? By this time he had calmed down; looking me fiercely in the eye, he said: 'It's this way, Ma'am. When yer lives in a village, yer 'ave to take wot yer can get.' There was a rumble of suppressed guffaws from the end of the room, which my loud coughing only just stopped in time.

The cruellest things of all were the anonymous letters to these poor chaps. Usually signed 'A friend' or 'A well-wisher', their filth and obscenity had to be read to be believed. I often wondered at the mentality of the writers – they were certainly not all from poor or illiterate people.

# 6

# ACROSS THE RHINE

Each morning after I had dressed Erna's neck wound, and before returning for breakfast, Roberts and I, on the trusty Mongrel, would do a 'tour' of the farms. We were issued with quite a lot of coffee, but only about one in every two hundred men asked for, or drank, it, since coffee drinking was not as popular then as it is now. So armed with a Carnation milk-tin of coffee or a few cigarettes, our shopping expeditions were very productive: eggs, chickens, the odd duck, home-made cheese, kohl rabi, fresh potatoes and, if we were lucky, a nice bit of freshly killed pork. The latter had to be handed over to Major Hopkins for analysis, as German pigs were very subject to a swine disease causing salmonella in humans. In return for his help, we would invite him to a lunch of roast pork, crackling, apple sauce, flowery potatoes boiled in their jackets, and kohl rabi. Thompson made a Yorkshire pudding like the 'wee folks' crispy pancakes' when he had fresh eggs. I would pay 'courtesy' visits to 'recovery', my bosom enlarged on the way out by the odd tin of fruit which Thompson converted into super flans. We did not always 'dine' so well, but nearly always had farm-fresh eggs and fresh vegetables. All highly illegal, but good clean fun and food.

Breaking up kindling one day by stamping my heel on it, I tore my Achilles' tendon and was unable to put my heel on the ground. Colin Mackenzie, the Second-in-Command of the 18 FDS saw me hobbling around and pounced on me. He dragged me up to the FDS, popping me into a walking plaster so I could go about my business. I cannot remember the other MOs names, but they were a great bunch of tireless, dedicated men (there were no nurses here at the front, the nearest being at the Head Unit, about twenty kilometres back). They and the reception area looked like a butcher's shop, as the wounded men were brought in. Unlike their French counterparts, the actual operating area and recovery tents were run with the clinical calmness, order and cleanliness of the best London hospitals.

Colin showed me two 'bomb happies' whom they could not 'break'. All my life I had heard that horses smelt fear. Nervous people seemed to exude it, and that was why horses played them up. Now I smelt it from these two men: they were cold and rigid as corpses on a mortuary slab, eyes staring, their breathing most peculiar, as if they were trying to hold it. One was a very young rifleman, the other older. I stooped down to touch the boy, as Colin had asked me, saying: 'Stroke his hair and talk to him.' Suddenly the tears came and he started calling, 'Mummy, Mummy!' The staff were overjoyed; they had thought they were going to lose him. As instructed, I cuddled him for a few minutes; it was an extraordinary experience, the warmth seeming to come back into him as his limbs relaxed. They gave him a shot of something and wheeled him out to the recovery area.

After that, Colin sent for me on several occasions in the wee small hours. It was horrible to see those mutilated men being brought in, some dead, others past all human aid, but the care and gentleness in all that chaos was remarkable. When there was a lull in the flow of wounded, they turned their attention to the 'bomb happies'. To me it was an extraordinary sight to see a big, husky MO or orderly down beside one of these men, cuddling and talking to them, gentle as a mother, until they 'broke'; then a good cry, sometimes with words tumbling out about their fear, a shot in the arm and they would be packed off. Next day they would go to a base hospital to convalesce and be put on light duties.

One night they brought in a magnificent-looking young Oberlieu-tenant SS man, with both his legs shot off. He cursed and swore at the 'Englisch schwein-hunds', absolutely refusing their treatment. He was put out with very near hopeless cases, and as I passed he filled his mouth with spittle and with perfect aim spat at me, hitting me on the cheek. Poor chap, he was dead before I went back later on.

Colin was a good 'trick cyclist': we often had long talks about my warped mentality. A sad event in our Strasse illustrates what I mean. A convoy had gone up leaving a few breakdowns to follow. Two of these men were looking for the Y when a shell ripped down the street, its burst cutting one of the men literally in half. His truncated body was sitting against the house wall; he had his beret with its red hackle still on and a silly look on his face. The other man was alive, lying on his back in the gutter, bleeding profusely. I knew the truncated man was beyond aid, but as I stooped to talk to the other one my mind went back to Granny Georgie and my bath time. She used to get me soap 'impeys', which were in the shape of legless imps with leering faces and curly quiffs of (soap) hair. They came in packs of three – violet, verbena and rose-coloured. Why after all those years should forgotten childish things come to mind I don't know but for some reason I wanted to giggle.

The live man was a Lowland Scot by his accent. Taking my hand, he said, 'Dinna greet for me, lassie, I'm going hame to see ma mither. Gie us a wee kiss.' As I stooped to do so, he tried to sit up, and the most frightful haemorrhage gushed out of his mouth all over me. I laid him back and hoped he would be with his mother. When the stretcher party arrived, they found that his back had been completely ripped off him; why he had not died instantaneously they did not know. I recount this sad event to illustrate these extraordinary flashbacks in my mind in moments of great stress or sorrow. Colin said it was a type of escapism as I had, and still have, a frightful revulsion and fear of the dead and dying. Looking back on those events and what I was to see later, the sheer stark horror of it all lent an unreal, nightmarish aspect so that I can only remember it as a very bad dream.

After about six weeks, George Denis seconded to me one of his bakers, a Corporal Oakes, who had been a pastry cook in civilian life. With the aid of the trusty Canadians, he built a magnificent field oven against the outside wall of the store. The Y had provided me with several bags of flour, and the 'courtesy' visits to 'recovery' increased. Oakes was turning out wonderful jam tarts, apple turnovers and a type of Manchester cake that could be cut in slices for a week's supply. Egon Ronay had nothing on our cuisine; the fame of the canteen was spreading.

Then the wind changed, the fire under the field oven flared up, caught the straw dollies under the ridged tiles, and we had a full-scale job for the fire brigade. My great fear was that the way the wind was blowing, the fire would travel to the roof of the garage: if that happened, with its contents, not only would the canteen go up, but a pretty fair share of the BSD only just across the narrow street.

I tore up the rickety stairs, seized my precious field boots, bedroll and what I could grab, chucked them out of the window on to the street, grabbed the cash box and day-book and proceeded to the street to find the 'Canadian shift' who were coming on duty rather shaken. The CO remarked that it was one thing to be sniped at by the Germans, but you did not expect to be assaulted with the Leader's field boots – one had hit the poor man on the head, and not lightly, as the trees were still in them. Everyone dined out on that story for weeks. There was a saying that the Canadians were too tough for the Aussies. The Canadian CO reversed it, saying that the Irish women ought to run assault courses for the Army, since they would teach them a thing or two about unarmed combat. Sadly, that ended our haute cuisine, as T. T. forbade any more field ovens near the canteen; the fire hazard with all the mines was too great.

By now, thanks to the Brig, Captain Tookit and Co., the canteen equipment had increased, necessitating a few extra 'lifts', five in all: four would tow the two mobile generators, water carrier and field kitchen boiler, with Erna, the piano and other luxury items on the fifth. The time was coming near for a spearhead over the Rhine which required a little organisation for Erna's transportation and comfort, now her wound was healing reasonably well. Casually I discussed my needs with George Denis, in the Brig's presence, doing a detailed drawing of how I would need two bed underlays bolted together in front, the bars padded with Army blankets, then a drop-in slip-rail at the back, also padded, forming a type of crate for her. With the piano on one side and the sofas and armchairs on the other, her crate would be well wedged for the bumpy ride she was sure to have. This bit of draughtsmanship I did on George's day-book, knowing he would have to tear out the page.

Three days later the travelling crate arrived, absolutely spot-on. It was parked under the remains of the stairs. Some strange officers came in for an urn of tea for their men stranded in a breakdown some way off, and seeing this, enquired what it was for. Charles Beach, a Major in 71 Group Pioneer Corps, was in the kitchen at the time; without a blink he said, 'Oh, we keep that for the CO when he goes mad.' The three strangers were still no wiser.

Frank Upton was a tower of strength over Erna, supplying her fodder. One captured German transport depot had horse rations in it. These were packs about two feet square of dehydrated oats, bran, soya and some finely chopped hay, heavily wrapped in brown paper

65

and marked off in foot squares, about the thickness and size of a single concrete brick. You broke a section off and when steeped in water it swelled into a wonderful mash. One brick was supposed to feed a horse for forty-eight hours. Frank brought these for Erna's hard-tack travelling rations and had a load of them reserved for her future requirements. He also got typed out (I still have them) her requisition papers in quadruple. I bet the Town Major had another headache over her. The old farmer got a tin of coffee plus 500 cigarettes and a box of cheroots all worth about £25, so he did not do too badly.

T. T. thought he would be very crafty by ordering five Scammels for my convoy. Scammels are on a big chassis, wide-based, with very little headroom, and each takes a five-ton lift. The jungle drums tipped me off about this so, equally craftily, when T. T. had left to go forward, I nipped down to the transport officer. Smiling as I hoped very sweetly, I said I would swop him a five-ton lift for a three, since the three-ton lorries had more headroom. At this time every ounce of lift was at a premium, supplies were being pushed over the Rhine for the spearhead like nobody's business. The poor transport officer thought this woman 'barmy' but gladly accepted the offer. As I was leaving the office, having got the order in my grubby little paw, I asked if he could organise a country boy as driver. With that request the poor man was sure I was heading for the loony bin.

At 5 am the following day, all four Scammels were loaded, their various trailers attached, the piano, sofas etc. all in situ, Erna's frame and rations in place, and she was coming down the road under armed escort. I went in the three-tonner to the station cattle-loading ramp, so all was in readiness to get her into the lorry. Oh boy! Did she play us up. It ended by her being lifted in bodily: once in her pen, eating hay, she was cheerful as a cricket, and she led the convoy. My instructions were to hide in one of the lorries before we came to the sentry on the Bailey bridge. We were trundling along merrily, going through Xantan, when there was an awful hullabaloo outside the Rathaus, a nice building with marble steps leading up to a large marble hall, round which swept a very fine curved staircase. We were liable for law and order until the 30 Corps Town Majors etc. appeared on the scene, and I do not think Military Government had been invented at this stage, so, as I was the only thing resembling a British officer, it fell to my lot to investigate the terrible murder of the Burgomeister, whose blood was running down the steps.

Organising my two guards, my hand inside my battledress on my trusty friend, I advanced. Somehow the blood looked odd, which made me suspicious that it was a trap, but I was assured that there had been a terrific explosion in the Rathaus. Kicking the badly shattered glass door open, what we found sent us into hoots of laughter – Frau and Herr Burgomeister had had one hell of a domestic row. She had aimed a near carboy-sized jar of pickled beetroot at him from the stairs, and either he was too nippy or her aim was rotten, for it had crashed about twenty feet away over the marble floor! As it was only a matter of days since the fighting round there had ceased, the townsfolk's nerves were still a bit jittery, so they had feared the worst when they heard a bang like that in the early morning.

As we were getting near the actual crossing, I nipped out to Erna's lorry, settling down on my bedroll in front of her.

I heard the sentry enquire what the convoy contained. Roberts, well spruced, said, 'Catering and welfare supplies.' We moved on, the lorry tipped forward and we hit the Bailey bridge, going swing, swing, clunketty bonk, clunketty bonk, I felt like calling out, 'Charing Cross Road! All change here!' as the swish of the brakes and upward tilt told me we were across.

Poor Erna had two terrors all her life – water and sheep. Halfway across the Rhine she started to bawl, and nothing I could do would stop her. The sentry on the landing side naturally asked Roberts what was the row? Cool as a trout, Roberts piped up: 'It's m'officer's charger, never did like crossing Bailey bridges.' The driver slipped into gear and we were in. I was believed to be the first civilian British female to cross the Rhine, which I am doubtful about, but certainly I was the first to cross it with my own horse. It was sad not to have been able to see our progress, but then one cannot have everything in this life.

Once across the Rhine we were all given very strict orders not to enter unoccupied houses, barns or stables, as there was a type of Maquis operating called 'Wer Wolves', one of whose more charming tricks was to string a steel wire across the road at the level of a motor-cycle rider. It was said that several poor despatch riders had been decapitated in this way.

Progress was extremely slow owing to shell-holes in the roads and the uncollected mines. The spearhead had gone through so fast, with stores being rushed up, that the mines were just taped off or stacked on the verges. The convoy in front of us was a big one but gradually pulled away. Behind us were two convoys, one a REME stores of about ten vehicles and behind that about fifteen vehicles, though what they were I cannot remember.

About fifteen kilometres in we went through a small forest. Pockets of Germans were still there at either side of the road and inclined to be impertinent in the way they sniped at us. Only because I was sitting down in front of Erna, who had bent her head down to me, were we saved from having 'bought it'. A bullet went through the canvas of the truck just where my head would have been. Erna's right ear was nicked – her third battle scar, which she was to carry to the day she was laid to rest in Tipperary twenty-six years later.

Coming out of the forest we were in very open, flat land, so we decided to 'brew up'. We were very popular with the other convoys for all we had to do was lift the smoke-stack of our boiler/kitchen and fan the embers – Thompson had stoked it up well and brought a bag of coal and coke with us. We had a good supply of hard-boiled eggs, tins of bully beef and nice fresh bread and butter. 'Recovery' had been paid extra 'courtesy calls', so we also had a kitty of self-heating soup, though this was for our own use in emergencies only. The land round us had the well-brushed and combed look of a good estate and there did not seem to be too much damage done to houses, trees or hedges.

About eight kilometres on we could hear machine guns stuttering and the odd crash of heavier artillery. A despatch rider came down from that direction, telling us that fighting had broken out again ahead of us. The previous convoy had been shelled and was caught in crossfire, but he thought it would be all over by the morning.

On our left was a very big park-like field with a hard metalled road running up to a fair-sized brick building. These were often used to store crops of hay etc. on the bigger estates. The REME NCO was a reasonable chap and fell in with my suggestion that although against orders, the barn would be the safest place to 'bivvie' for the night. Oddly untouched, it had plenty of clean straw and, greatest of all joys, a standpipe with clean water in it. From the fine brown dust we all looked exactly like the advertisements for the old-fashioned Monkey Brand Knife Cleaning Powder. The dust was exactly like it too. It seeped into everything, even your mouth.

We mounted a patrolling guard for the night and unloaded Erna, tying her up at my end of the barn, the men kipping down at the door end. Dead beat, clean and well fed, we all fell asleep nearly at once, except the guard. Suddenly, I awoke, feeling a heavy weight on my chest and something woolly being forced into my mouth. Wer Wolves was my first thought, yelling as best I could. The guards came in with their dim torches, and the others in various stages of undress converged on me, to see Erna lying down contentedly beside me with her head on my chest and an ear nearly in my mouth. She had undone her rope and strolled over to be 'companionable like'. Like myself, the lads didn't know if they wanted to shoot her for the fright she gave us all or hug her for not being a Wer Wolf.

By morning, the gunfire had died down, so we hit the road about 6.30 am, eventually getting through to Bergsteinfurt about 4.30 pm, again in our Monkey Brand camouflage. All these past weeks and months since 'Deirdre of the Sorrows', my ex-colleague, had been returned to base, the only English woman I had seen or spoken to, and that only once, was my distant cousin, Vanessa who had left the Free French and was driving a Forward Stores supply lorry. She was a marvel, never letting any of the Forward Area tea-cars or my outfit down. If she was turned back on one route, she would try another, and to get up to the lines she smeared her face with axle grease – being very tall and wearing many layers of clothes, regulation issue boots and gaiters, she could easily pass for a man, even making her upper-crust English accent into a deep growl of soldier's lingo.

As I was giving my report to T. T. on arrival in Bergsteinfurt, one hell of a fracas started in the orderly room next door. A very upper-crust female accent was shouting far from upper-crust remarks that she was a Y driver, my cousin, and had brought me stores, also that if their 'Old Man' (the CO) was so bloody-minded that they had put her under arrest, he b— well didn't deserve a canteen. T. T. raised an eyebrow and asked if I knew what was going on.

'Not exactly, but it is Vanessa's voice, and she is due with stores for me.'

'Staff!' he called, 'bring in your prisoner.' He had never seen her before.

Her first greeting to me was: 'Really, you *are* a bitch. I had one hell of a job to find you and then these b—s tried to clap me in irons.'

Telling her to shut up, and did she want me to leave rice on the road like the Babes in the Wood, she smartly replied: 'Well, you could have left one of your Irish tinker's marks. They would fox any b—Jerry.'

While this affectionate cousinly exchange was taking place, poor T. T. was looking a trifle bewildered, trying to assess the 'prisoner'. At last he said: 'You both look as if you could do with a drink.' Then Vanessa did her *pièce de résistance* by starting to divest herself: first off came the loose camouflage jacket, then a thick muffler, followed by, if my memory serves me correctly, a flying officer's sheepskin jacket, then Army issue battledress, blouse and trousers about six sizes too big for her, then a heavy polo-neck sweater under which she had a very respectable, well-fitting battledress, shirt, collar and tie. By the time she got down to basics T. T. had given up the unequal struggle of being the strict CO and had dissolved into hysterics.

Joking aside, she was superb at her job. Strong as an ox, heart of a lion and nerves of steel, she often got cut off by enemy action and would sleep in her truck. Nor was she afraid to use her gun. One night she was perforce sleeping out and was attacked by two GIs: they will think twice before trying it on another English woman, I imagine. An amusing tale, also true, about her, which she had already told me, was told by the poor transport officer I conned into breaking orders and giving me a three-ton lift. We were at a party in Herford shortly before we went home, given by my old CRE, Arthur Villiers, now up-graded a few pips, and his wife, who was a first cousin of Vanessa's mother Bertie. Vanessa and I turned up in our 'little black dresses' and were having great crack with some of the sappers, singing and dancing the CRE song. The transport officer turned to Arthur, saying: 'Do you see those two civilians? They are the biggest pair of bitches unhung. The big one would twist your neck, but the little one [me] is dangerous; a bloody sly one.' Much amused, Arthur told him we were cousins and that the 'little one' was schooled by one of the best brains that ever came out of Camberley Staff College, i.e. Chipps. The poor TO had got a rocket over me, but dared not report the Vanessa episode.

Somewhere down near Wuppertal, where there was quite a bit of fighting, the camb shaft had gone on her lorry, which was full of stores for the Forward mobiles. She stopped an empty lorry coming back, and at gunpoint got the driver and his mate to load his lorry with Y stores. She drove off in it, leaving instructions to have *her* lorry repaired and that she would pick it up in three days. Good as her word, she returned the ambushed lorry to the depot and collected her own. The TO tried to get her on the carpet but she blithely informed him he had nothing to complain about as his lorry was in *perfect running order* except for six bullet holes, a broken side window and the roof torn where the branch of a tree fell on it. She thanked him very nicely for the loan of it, 'swept' out and collected the repaired Y lorry. No wonder the poor chap asked Arthur if they bred any more like us two in Ireland!

When Vanessa related this story to me, she ended by remarking that she did not know what he had to complain about as the engine and the tyres were perfectly OK when she handed the lorry back. She did Trojan work for the Y all the way along, and never even got a thank-you. Any of the Forward Leaders still alive will bear out what I say. She knew instinctively when and what you would be running short of, even if your indent had not got through to Diest or Leopoldsville, whichever of the stores she was operating from. She had a very tough assignment which she never shirked. Sadly, both she and Bertie have now gone to their reward.

# 7

# THE LAST LAP TO PEACE

It was on the way up to Burgsteinfurt, going through the ruins of Bocholt, that my love affair with Dobermann Pinschers started.

In front of the convoy a most beautiful, elegant, black-and-tan hound stalked out of the rubble of a factory: he stood like the Monarch of the Glen surveying us, his coat shining, muscles rippling, a veritable prince of the dog world. Though his tail was docked, his ears were not. Having made his presence felt, he moved across the road, graciously allowing us to pass. I was hooked. No one could tell me what type of dog he was.

At Burgsteinfurt the BSD was installed in a brewery. Erna had a super stable with an automatic drinking bowl and I used the one next door for my 'clinic'. We had to put a notice on her door, 'Please do not feed me', as the boys were potty about her, giving her chocolate and sweets of all kinds. When Roberts found her with a mouthful of Wrigley's spearmint, we had a major dental operation to get it out of the few teeth she had – we felt enough was enough.

Exercising her round the town under armed guard, the reaction of the local women was very interesting: some clapped, cheered, and even curtsied to us; others spat on the ground. The most violent reaction of all was when I went out in the full correct Y uniform. This I found on the rest of the way up, and it was explained to me by an interpreter. Whilst I was in khaki battledress, I belonged to the British Army, and they knew the British would not bring a woman into danger: therefore the war was as good as over and their menfolk would soon be home. The greyish-blue of the Y uniform, however, was exactly like that of the women attached to the German forces, derisively known as the 'Grey Mice'. These women were loathed by the civilian population and looked upon as more dangerous than the SS. What their mission in life was I never really understood, but they apparently were very highly trained, using their 'female wiles' to 'shop' people to the powers-that-be. Hence the spitting and garbage thrown at me.

Two days after we arrived, two letters in English arrived for the CO and me, coming from an old English lady who lived in a fairy-tale moated *schloss* a little way outside the town. Would I please go to tea with her with the CO's permission? She was the widow of a Baron, who was one of the old German aristocracy, nearly Royal, the daughter of an English aristocrat and the grand-daughter of a titled West of Ireland family. She had married her Baron in 1908 and during the 1914–18 War her British relatives cut her off from the family, having nothing to do with her ever afterwards. The CO checked her out, and I was permitted to go with an armed escort of six men plus Roberts, who were detailed not to let me out of their sight.

The *schloss* had a dry moat round it, in which were little shelters with deep straw inside, and about fifteen magnificent Dobermann Pinschers, *all* with their tails on. I was still enraptured at this sight when the great doors were swung open by a decrepit retainer. The *schloss* was built round a courtyard across which we were taken to the most magnificent hall hung with every conceivable hunting trophy: it had stepped straight out of Grimms' brothers. Down the wide stairs came a very English Old Lady. Her outrider was an elderly white bull terrier, her bodyguard six magnificent 'Dobies', all with ears and tails on.

Every bull terrier person knows that bull terrier addicts and bull terriers have an affinity. Before anything was said, Bill the Bully, for that was his name, charged me. I was on my knees hugging him: the old lady was laughing and crying at the same time. The Dobies had surrounded us and were licking me in that peculiarly gentle way of their breed, with their very dry, velvety tongues. It was a very emotional scene. The Baroness spoke English with a marked German accent. She gave me some horrible herb tea and very Germanic cake, and did we talk bull terriers and Dobies! She believed it was they who had protected her and her feeble old husband, as much as the fact that most of the townspeople and surrounding farmers were loyal to his family. He had died in the second year of the war, they had no family, he was the last of his, so she was alone except for her dogs and three very old retainers. She and her husband had bought Bill on their last trip to England before war broke out. She told me that her family ignored her completely:

73

when in London, she said, 'We were like foreign tourists.' The
Baron must have been a fine looking man from his photograph. He
had a real duelling scar, *not* the *nouveau riche* effort done at great
expense by a plastic surgeon.

From then on I wanted a Dobermann Pinscher as a second string
to my beloved bull terriers. I had to wait thirty-five years before my
beloved Grainnia arrived. She was my most delightful, devoted
friend and companion for three years, to be taken from me by the
dreadful spondalitis which is so prevalent in the Irish-bred
Dobermanns.

We were only a few days in Burgsteinfurt before moving up to
Hanover. While we were in Hanover, the BSD was in a large
concrete jungle of a German barracks and depot east of the city.
The Russians had passed Magdeburg, coming right up to the British
sector. The whole line was in a state of chaotic flux, with Russian
and British vehicles in the same compound.

The ordinary 'Rooski' soldiers were ill-clad, ill-fed and very dirty,
and practically none of them could read. We had to show our passes
to get about this area, and the only response we got from the great
unwashed as they looked at the pages upside down, turning them
by licking a filthy thumb, was, 'Nicht, nicht,' grunted at us. Sitting
in our adjutant's office, idly watching the Russians milling about
below in the compound, I saw an officer draw his gun and shoot one
of his own men for failing to salute. He gave him a kick and with
his thumb indicated to an NCO that the dead man was to be moved.
He was still there when we left about an hour later.

In the last mad push towards Berlin and Magdeburg, the Russians
were out of provisions as we knew them, actually living off the land
like locusts, sacking the villages and farms for food and crucifying
many of the inhabitants upside down on their own doors, trees and
outhouses. Colin Mackenzie and 18 DS were then just outside
Magdeburg and he took me to a village nearby which had been
sacked by the Russians. They had stripped all the inhabitants naked
– men, women and children – made them put straw in what looked
to me like a great tithe barn, sprinkled the straw with petrol, drove
them into it like cattle, secured the great doors, and set it alight by
firing tracer bullets into it. When each batch was burned, they
repeated the process. The British had captured photographs of these
events taken by Russian officers. The Russians had also raped the
women, both young and old, whilst they waited their turn to be

burned. As one medical orderly said: 'These are supposed to be our Gallant Allies'. Colin took me to see the shell of the barn; it was waist-deep in charred human remains and bones. Shortly afterwards, the Russian line was pushed back and stabilised, much to the chagrin of the local people, whose villages they had already passed through once. The events related here were only minor incidents, mostly swept under the carpet.

While we were in Hanover, Belsen, about sixteen kilometres away, was liberated. The only rations issued from the Daily Issue Depot serving Belsen were chicken broth, Complan and invalid foods. Belsen, situated equi-distant between Soltau and Celle, had, next to its atrocities, a German veterinary and fodder store for cavalry and horse transport. There was the most up-to-date veterinary equipment as well as drugs, yet the by now sub-humans next door got nothing of it. The adjutant took me to it to collect what I needed for Erna. This was ten days after the Belsen liberation, and the stench from it was so awful that I could not spend much time in the veterinary store. When questioned about Belsen, the locals in Saltau and Celle said they understood it was a veterinary hospital! With the lorry-loads of human cattle going into it and the overpowering smell of death, how they could imagine their story would be accepted is incredible.

Fritz Renton had the awful job of supplying Pioneers and labour to try to clear it. There is no need for me to go into details, since it has already been so well documented. When he took me round it, we wore surgical masks. You literally could not tell the living from the dead; they mostly looked like parchment stretched over wooden frames. In one pile of dead, the mouths were gaping holes where the gold had been extracted from their teeth. There had also been (not surprisingly) quite a bit of cannabalism, and some of the skeletal babies were ripped open with their livers torn out. The local women were brought in to help to clean up and bury the dead: some, for a joke, planted them in a row, heads and feet sticking up alternately. Fritz saw red at this: he ordered every able-bodied woman in the district to dress in their best ceremonial native costumes (which were very beautiful) to pay respect to the dead they were burying. As he spoke German as fluently as English, they knew they could not fool him. Writing this, I can smell the horror of it. There was one peculiar thing: the officers in charge and the soldiers who had to do such grizzly work handling and burying the dead, never got any terrible diseases out of it or the other camps, with very rare exceptions, but the medical students, doctors and nurses sent out from the UK to cope with the awful situation picked up all the bugs that could be collected, despite having every possible protective inoculation before leaving home. A hospital matron explained it to me afterwards, saying: 'You all had built up your own immunity in all the filth on the way up. These people were like the buxom fresh country girls I'd get as student nurses, who would go down with every infection they could get, whilst the city girls were immune.'

In Hanover, the adjutant had billeted me in a small suburban villa with Erna just down the road with a dairy farmer. Her stall was next to a delightful Bavarian working ox, whom she eyed with grave suspicion. He, in his mild and gentle way, eyed her with interest and a puzzled look on his face as he chewed his cud.

There was also, more dangerous to anyone's life and limb, a Polish refugee camp between Hanover and my billet. They were a dreadful rabble, completely lawless, ruthless and undisciplined and had to be kept under close surveillance, as no property or person was safe from them, the women as fiercely savage as were the men. On our second day there, Roberts, who had been billeted with me, went down before breakfast to feed Erna and met the dairy farmer tearing up the strasse to say that the Poles had taken Erna and his ox to slaughter them, holding him at knifepoint. Roberts kept his head, grabbed a few British Tommies who were on their way to their respective jobs, told them to get the mare and ox and came flying back for me. We caught up with them as they were just taking Erna and the ox into their compound: I told my posse to fix bayonets, drew my sidearm and put the leaders under arrest – which I had no authority to do. Roberts took Erna, the farmer his ox, and I literally drove the ringleaders down to our HQ; the bewildered Tommies, nothing loth, thought it was all good clean fun. Hands over their heads, the Poles were marched into 27 CRASC HQ, which was in part of the old Winter Palace in Hanover. The big white horse on his pedestal must have had a private smile. Frank Upton, who was on duty, put the Poles under proper arrest and then, for the only time in all the years I knew him, lost his temper when the leader said he did not know what all the fuss was about as the horse was a woman's, women were only useful for one thing, had no rights and that he and his brothers were starving. This was quite untrue as they were very well vittled indeed, both by Army and civilian standards.

The dairy farmer and his family could not do enough for Roberts and me during the remaining few days we were there. He was given a guard for his stock. Every time we passed the compound, the Poles hurled obscenities at Roberts and me. I heard afterwards that they knifed the Military Government Camp Warden and shot his Second-in-Command, disposing of them no one knew where. Erna and the ox must have led charmed lives.

After a week in Hanover, 27 CRASC went back down 240 Up to Freistett with 56 BSD, working in the store houses of a big commune known locally as 'The Hospital', which I gathered was for mentally deficient boys of all ages. The Warden was an arrogant, fat bully: he and his staff were hated by the local farmers and residents in the Freistett area.

The country round Freistett was flat, with heavy, dark clay like the Lincolnshihre Fens and parts of Holland in East Anglia. There would be the most wonderful sheet lightning at night (those who had good cameras took photographs of it), and there were myriads of frogs of all descriptions. The croaking of the big bull-frogs at night, with the croak and wheeze of a type of toad, lulled one to sleep like a muted orchestra.

For the first three days at Freistett, Erna and I literally lived in HQ Mess, she in the over-grown garden at the back by day, with a large shed as a stable at night.

By this time she was badly in need of a blacksmith. Just up the road from the Mess was a blacksmith's shop. To me it was like Aladdin's Cave. Never had I seen such wonderful ultra-modern electrical equipment in any blacksmith's: then came a rude awakening. The shoes were so thick they would have very well stood in for narrow-gauge railway lines and would certainly have been excellent in schooling Hackneys to lift their feet up. There were two men to do the actual shoeing, a third as a type of plumber's tiger to hand nails, like junior crowbars, and switch on the different electrical gadgets. If this was only a tiny country forge out in the wilds, what would a bigger establishment's equipment be like?

One man held up Erna's leg whilst the other fitted the shoe, the third handed the nails, rasp or searching knife, a barbarous looking affair compared with ours. Each hoof was finished off completely, laced and rasped before the next one was shod, the leg holder placing the hoof on a tripod – now in common use in the UK – whilst the smith laced the clinches. After 3½ hours, for the price of 1½ Reichsmarks (3/9d in old money), poor Erna clumped out of the forge and down to her back garden, the two of us utterly exhausted.

It was in Freistett whilst searching for another 'desirable residence', that I had my brush with three Panzer tanks about to go into action. There was a village hall, we were told, that had all mod. cons. And a house, so I took a short cut. A small convoy was pulled up by the roadside as Roberts and I whizzed by on the Mongrel. A very young lieutenant halted me, was scared out of his wits when he saw it was a female on the bike, stuttered and stumbled, and told me it would not be very wise to go round there, indicating the corner in front. Airily I brushed him to one side, with the remark that it was there that the village hall was. Roberts pushed, and we were off. Round the bend, guns trained full on us and the crossroads behind us, were three Panzer tanks. Behind them the road widened and looked clear. I must add here that the Mongrel's silencer was conspicuous by its absence; when on full throttle it would burst your eardrums. I waved to the Germans, gave the Mongrel all the juice it could take, passed the three tanks, did a nifty U-turn, nearly unshipping poor Roberts, waved merrily to them as we roared past them again and disappeared in a cloud of dust. I did not have time to study their facial expressions, but Roberts told me they were all gaping with their mouths open. After a few warning shots, they surrendered in about an hour. T. T. said it was the racket from the Mongrel that had unnerved them!

The canteen at Freistett was a long, low farm cottage-type house on the roadside. We requisitioned it semi-furnished – it even had curtains which were quite gay, so no need for Mickey Mouse. It also sported a bathroom with a geyser heated by machine-dried turf. Erna had a good stable and an enclosed field of about ten acres, so we were all living in luxury. The German POWs were coming down the road in shoals, many of their lorries driven by themselves. They waved, cheered and gave the V-sign; most of them were singing 'Lili Marleen'. When the Canadian and British forces joined in a pincer operation, we got a whole infantry battalion coming down the road in full retreat, literally looking for the POW camps. Standing at the garden gate for some time watching them pass, I was reminded of my childhood when the IRA passed my old home one August evening in 1922.

These German soldiers, who had been highly trained and were at one time the pride of their nation, were in equal disarray to the IRA, their uniforms ragged, in some instances no boots on their feet. They had come a very long way. It was significant that there did not seem to be any men in the 20–35 age group. They were either very young boys or men well over 40, which showed that Hitler was scraping the barrel for recruits.

Next down the road came the unfortunates who could be transferred from Belsen, standing packed like cattle in the lorries, dressed in their awful striped prison clothes, on their way to the cleansing and rehabilitation centres where they would be sorted, categorised, or labelled as displaced persons. With their shaven heads and skull-like grinning faces, they were pitiable objects. It seems incredible, but when a convoy of these poor things was coming down the road, if the wind was behind them you got the awful sickly stench of death about half a mile in advance of them. We learned to rush around and close all the canteen windows, because after the first lot went by it permeated the whole building and was impossible to get rid of for hours afterwards.

The next travellers to pass our way were the refugees from the 'Rooskies', whole families with their possessions piled on the long German carts, usually surmounted by Grandma in full national costume and the younger children with either kittens or puppies in their arms. If they were well off, they might have two or three horses or mules or an ox, sometimes a mixture, pulling these carts. One of these wagons of human tragedy was pulled by a dreadful weak old horse: as he got level with the canteen he dropped, tipping Grandma and a little girl who had a tiny fawn in her arms off on to the road.

The old man gave the dead horse a kick, shrugged his shoulders, ordered his other womenfolk to take off the tackling and shoved the laden cart back. It had a pole, so I presume they may have had two horses or an ox when they started. They had come from the Russian zone near Magdeburg. He calmly took off the horse's bridle and adjourned into Erna's field. His intentions were obvious, but needless to say, like all good ones, they ended as paving stones to hell! I sent for the head of the commune, ordering him to remove cart and horse and saying that should anything happen to Erna, he

would be shot out of hand. He brought about fifty of the poor
mental defectives who lived and worked in the commune. I gave the
little fawn some Complan, which it drank eagerly. Afterwards I was
told that the head man had ordered the horse to be skinned and fed
it to the inmates. It was so old and thin they must have used
hacksaws to cut it up.

All the locals lived in terror of the 'Rooskies': these were the
Russian POW's doled out to the farmers as labourers. When they
knew the game was up and Germany licked, they turned quite
nasty, some raping, murdering and even setting fire to their
erstwhile employers' houses. We were still responsible for law and
order, and our troops were often called out to these cases.

Just up the road a quiet old couple of simple country folk lived
on their tiny farm: they were of the old school, hating the Hitler
regime, also the commune and those that ran it. They took great
interest in my *'cranken pferd'* (sick horse). Their dogs were well
cared for, as were their one ox and milch cow who pulled their
timber plough.

We were just opening for the morning session when the old
woman came tearing down the road screaming: *'Mein man kaput,
Rooskie, Rooskie! Mein man kaput!'* Taking a few boys with me, I
found the poor old man with a four-prong fork in his stomach,
waving about like a tuning fork, he being strung up to a tree in their
yard. The Rooskie was no Pierpoint, so his hangmanship was not
very expert. We cut the poor old boy down and sent for an MO and
blood wagon, into which he was eventually transferred, the fork still
*in situ*. About ten days later he came to thank me, bearing vegetables
for us and freshly-cut lucerne for Erna. Whilst we were there, she
never wanted for anything. Roberts said it was like the fairies –
every morning there was either hay, straw, roots or something
outside her door.

Two days before Bremen and Hamburg were taken, towards the
end of April in 1945, the sky was black with aircraft. It was indeed
a wondrous sight. I think it was the Canadians as well as the RAF,
but the flying accuracy was superb. They converged on both cities
at what I can only describe as a cross on four levels, like well-trained
infantry marching and counter-marching. They told us afterwards
that when Bremen and Hamburg surrendered, not a shot was fired,
our troops just walked in. Fritz took me to see Hamburg a few days
afterwards. The streets were still blazing, the city in rubble, and

many people were unable to get out of their cellars because of the blazing tar on the streets.

When peace broke out, the whole HQ was dispersed, scattered like chaff in the wind, and the BSD wound down, with only a few officers and men to keep it ticking.

Fritz Renton's HQ was then at Sulingen, about ten kilometres up the road, and he applied for my canteen. We had a large but rather gloomy house, which had been used as a beer garden, and civilian labour, which was a great joy. Erna and I again lived in the Pioneer HQ Mess; she had a nice box at the back of the house. The bugler, who had been a stableman in civvy street, was detailed to look after her, taking her out to the Army sports ground, where she grazed, and bringing her back about 5 pm every day.

She had several cookhouse ports of call on the way for her favourite delicacy – bread and margarine dipped in sugar – and would not pass them until she got it. Just on the outskirts of the town was an excellent Der Ronditors, who made the most lovely *apfel strudel* which all the lads were very fond of, especially the bugler. He had one on his way back with Erna every evening, sharing it with her.

All was well until he went on leave. I was away for the day and late back. Fritz had a Top Brass – very Top and Extra Brass – conference on, when a terrified NCO literally burst into the conference with, 'Ma'am's mare has gone!'

'Well, find her!'

As the conference drew to a close, two even more agitated NCOs arrived: 'We found the mare, Sir, but she's stuck in the pastrycook's shop and won't come out for us.' Fritz was the only horsey man in HQ, and a particular friend of Erna's as he always carried a packet of pear drops, to which both of them were addicted. Armed with these, a lead rein, a brace of generals, brigadiers and colonels, Fritz sallied forth to capture the terrible beast in the pastrycook's. When his posse arrived, she was standing quite quietly in the narrow shop, finishing off the last lot of pastry on display in the window. Fritz calmly pushed past her, clipped on her lead rein and backed her out of the shop. The owner and his family, plus bystanders, thought it was the bravest thing they had ever seen. It made all the Brass Hats' day – most of the Senior Pioneers' Officers were ex-cavalrymen like Fritz. Work for the day over, they thoroughly enjoyed the joke and, in true cavalry style, 'made much' of the now very sticky Erna.

Never again did she have such a grand and splendid escort back to her box: a 'brace' of generals, a 'wisp' of brigadiers and a 'charm' of colonels!

The trouble had started by her 'stand in' groom being late to collect her. Bored with waiting, she had opened her gate, progressing towards her stable via the cookhouses, but, grabbing her titbit, she belted off and would not let anyone catch her. Gluttony and the narrowness of the pastry shop were her undoing.

# 8

# HQ Mess

Bob (Robbie) Roberts, the YMCA Second-in-Command, came up to ask if I would finish out my time by running the Y HQ Mess at Bad Salzuflen, where all the Council of Voluntary War Workers HQs had moved. He arranged accommodation for Erna and allowed my poor batman Roberts to come to settle us in. Regretfully, the Mongrel was handed back to REME, but I was promoted to a decrepit jeep known as 'Minnie Mouse'. No one else at HQ would drive it. It had been in several smashes and its chassis was out of alignment, but with care and attention it conveyed me on many nefarious occasions until my time was up.

Fritz Renton was very kind to me all the way up, and could make Bill Laing jump a foot into the air because he was a full Colonel with a chest of medals, from both wars, equal to any General. He sent his adjutant one day to collect me to take me on a 'swan'. We did not inform Y HQ that it was to the Potsdam Conference. The thing that stands out in my mind most was the careless and gay way Winston Churchill sat up in his jeep for all to see, cigar in mouth and giving the V-sign. Naturally there was very high security around him, but Joe Stalin was more like toothpaste in a tube, being squeezed out of his bullet-proof car between a triple row of security guards into the conference building. In his photographs he gave the impression of being a much bigger man. When he looked at you, his cold snake's eyes in their Slavonic setting never smiled, though the rest of his face crinkled in the right places.

When I was in Attleborough I had met the American General Mark Clarke. He had heard about Erna, and called to see me in Bad Salzuflen, inviting me to the special performance of the famous Lippizaners of the Spanish Riding School who had been evacuated from their stud farm at Piber to Wels, now in the American sector. They put on a special show for Patton, Eisenhower and other VIPs at St Martin's, near the Austrian border. I never got to see them in their famous Vienna Riding School.

These odd 'swans', never more than about 18 hours off duty, were the only leave I got, except for three days to take Erna down to Stockel and Lens on the first leg of her journey home. On my return journey I had to bring a three-ton store van back to HQ. It was nearly clapped out, with leaking gaskets, and the diesel fumes from the engine, which was between the driver and passenger seats, nearly made me sick.

The whole of Malke Strassse in Bad Salzuflen inside the barrier was reserved for CVWW HQs, and the Y, being the largest of these bodies, had the most houses. The others managed with one house combining Mess, offices and transit hostel, with the exception of the Salvation Army. When I took over, we had four houses for Mess and general offices, one across the street lower down as our transit hostel, and a self-contained house with its own cook and civilian staff, all under my jurisdiction. Our street was known as 'Holy Row'.

Vanessa called the town 'Bad Smell Snuffling'. She only graced us with her presence under duress. We were not liked because we neither kowtowed nor conformed, getting on with our jobs, neither asking nor taking quarter from anyone. Once I suggested to our Queen Bee, Miss Harding, that she should instruct the new drafts out from the UK in the correct way to drink wine. I tried to suggest that they were unaccustomed to it owing to war-time shortages. (Not being like Adam Scott, I did not say that they were the type of girls who would not have wine with their meals at home.) She looked me in the eye, quite bluntly telling me to mind my own business. Frankly, that was precisely what I was doing, because my office-cum-bedroom was on the ground floor next to the ante-room. It was a very pleasant room with a lovely sunny balcony available when you had time to sit on it. The young ladies used to come in 'plastered' from wining and dining at the Officers Club in the Kur House, where the waters were taken, then in the wee small hours I would be yanked out of bed to either administer to the sick, undress the collapsed, or clean up the vomit in the hall or on the stairs – I did not like to leave it to the civilian staff, as I felt it would create a bad image of a supposed religious organisation. I also had to cover for the girls at breakfast time when they could not appear. I believe it was only Vanessa and one very excellent secretary who knew of these misadventures at midnight.

Having been well and truly snubbed, I solved my problem by removing my sleeping quarters to a fifth house which I had acquired. When 'Lord Leicester's spirit came a-scratching on the door', they found that Queen Bess had flown, and they had to cope on their own.

The 'Sally Ann' Brigadier's house, which I had acquired, was a great joke. Stupidly I wondered what a 'Brig' would be doing in 'Holy Row'. We were bursting at the seams for sleeping accommodation, and it seemed such a pity that the next house down was vacant, so with my trusty assistant Harry Hunt, we did a recce, getting in through a small back window. It was fully furnished except for bed linen. We consulted Robbie. Unfortunately, he being a fine big man was unable to avail himself of our private access route. The Town Majors had arrived – much maligned, 'troublesome' men but necessary evils – so I tackled one about the house. He hummed and ha'd, muttering about the Brigadier, so I let it cool for a day or two and then invited him to dinner at the Club.

In the meantime, the Sunday papers were full of the Brig's doings. Over our cigars and brandy, I returned to the attack. The TM was wavering: 'Of course,' he said, 'you could take possession of it if you could get in. But still, in the Brig's absence I don't feel justified in handing it over.' Then the *Sunday Express* played my trump card, grand slam and all. I suggested, producing a copy, that if he read the headlines he would see that owing to a little 'cash flow' problem, the Brig would not need a residence in BLA, as he would be staying as a guest in one of His Majesty's houses in the UK for some time. The cash flow of quite a few thousand pounds had gone down the wrong drain.

'My Gawd, who'd have thought it! You can have your house!' He brought me the key the next day.

I felt very sorry for all the members of the Sally Ann because they did a terrific job. Their canteens were always spotless, welcoming and cheerful. Any serviceman or woman will tell you that they had that little extra something that sparkled, making all the difference. I do not wish to be disloyal to the Y, but their canteens always reminded me of a dreary church on a wet day after a funeral, the vicar and verger trying to be Oh So Jolly to erase the sad event. The

Sally Ann's secret was that they were usually run by a cheerful husband-and-wife team.

After the acquisition of the Brig's house, Robbie, Alex Telfor, who drew the rations, Harry Hunt, our Forward Area Secretary Don Tyler, and I moved in with stealth. We left a spare room for what I called the 'outliers' such as George Upton and other 'Heads of State', a special room next to my own for our courier, Coco Bertouille, and a spare bed in my room for Vanessa, should she and Coco be with us at the same time. We also had a nice, well-furnished, sitting-room in which to entertain our own friends or have a quiet chat without the 'finny denizers' of the Mess snapping at our heels. Every four weeks a new draft would come out as replacements for the worn-out slaves being returned, mostly without thanks. On one of these drafts was the wife of a very famous then Brigadier, later to be titled and a full General. She had blue hair and a foghorn voice. First of all she had driven poor Coco nearly bonkers on the way up, criticising his vehicle and driving, and she had fought with the frontier guards, refusing to get out of the mini-bus for them or show her passport because she was Mrs X.

The drill in the transit hostel was that heavy luggage was left in a locked room on the ground floor, to which only Alex Telfor and I had keys. The new arrivals could choose their own room-mates, and this they did while in the highly ecstatic first flush of enthusiasm, only to fall out violently at a later date! That was not my problem. The rules were simple, a wash and brush-up, a nice hot meal, then they rested until tea at 4 pm. At 4.30 pm they were collected and taken across to Miss Harding and Bill Laing for interviews and posting, all strictly taken in alphabetical order.

Mrs X started by bawling at me from halfway up the stairs! 'Here, you!' Alex and I were dealing with the house list for rations and took no notice. She came at us like a rhinoceros. Did we know who *she* was? She was insisting upon a single room – none available. When the gong announced their meal she came down, sitting herself at the end of the table, and started to butter her roll. Coco, as the only male, had the other end, and stood to say Grace. He eyed me for his cue: very Sergeant-Majorish, I said, 'Will you all please stand while Monsieur Bertouille says Grace?' The others stood politely, all eyes turned on her; they had had a bellyful of her on the way up. Reluctantly she got to her feet. Grace hardly over, she turned to me.

'Don't you know who I am? I'm Brigadier X's wife.'

'Yes, that's his horrible luck, poor chap,' with which pleasantry I 'swep out'. Before this she had been snapping her fingers and shouting, 'Schnell, schnell' at the waitress, who quietly asked me to get the lady to speak English so she could understand her!

On Brigadier X's orders, the lady was to be posted as far as possible from his HQ. Next day she was 'deported' to Schleswig-Holstein.

Another very 'odd bod' was a tall, gaunt lady who was a professor of something-or-other and out to do either research or a summary of the work of the Y. Robbie called her his '*bête noire*'. She pursued everyone with questions and could clear the anteroom at tea time in three minutes flat. George Upton, Harry Hunt and Don Tyler were having a quiet chat and a mug of tea on my balcony when this dreaded lady burst into my room. Without any preamble she ordered a '*really* nice tea' to be served in the anteroom, as she had invited an SS Oberstleutnant to tea. She was promptly disabused of *that* idea, because although 'frat' was allowed, these men were not permitted inside our barriers. It was a good thing I was sitting down, for her next remark: 'Oh! But he must come to tea! I am going to sleep with him and want you to arrange a room for us!' Taking a deep breath, I told her to go and see Miss Harding, who took care of all these things, as I had nothing to do with the moral welfare of the staff, but bring an SS man into our mess she would *not*. The three heroes on the balcony were convulsed, one of them remarking: 'He'd want more than SS training to take her on.' We never knew if she did go to Miss Harding, because to get anything out of that lady was, as some wag said, like trying to open an oyster with a discarded drinking straw. But I rather fancy she did, for Miss Harding eyed me in a very suspiciously contemplative way for the next few days.

More women were coming out to BLA now, in various capacities, including quite a lot of young war widows. I was so sorry for them; they nearly all reminded me of kittens in a pet shop, with their wide, sad eyes and little pinched faces, anxiously scanning every passer-by hoping for a good home and/or a kindly master. I realised how they must have felt, but on the other hand their marriages, hopefully happy, would have been of a very short duration and in time would fade into just a very lovely '*affaire*'. The wives of regular soldiers, with long, very happy marriages of trust and companionship, like myself, might accept the loss of their husbands in one way, but would find the gaping hole in their lives harder to fill in peacetime. There was no good in allowing myself to wallow in self-pity for I was going back to marry a very dear and special friend of many years' standing.

The bulldozer of peace had crashed through the barriers of team spirit and comradeship, trailing tentacles of red tape, infighting and petty bickering in its wake. It is a sobering thought that it takes a war to bring out the best in people. There was a supportive feeling of interdependence on each other in the way masons of old built those lovely stone arches without cement or mortar, each stone keeping the other in place. But with every unit reorganised in a general shake-up, this camaraderie was shattered. Everyone was tired, the nervous tension that keyed us up was gone, and with it and deflation came the winter of discontent and a Labour Government.

The only hope I had in the latter was that they might do something about soldiers' widows' pensions which were and still are a disgrace to any nation. It is a positive insult, that such a pittance should be allotted to women whose husbands and family breadwinners gave their lives for their country. The letters I had received from widows of all ranks on this subject were heart-breaking, and men going forward had often broached it to me, their one fear if they were killed being that their families would be living well below the subsistence level. The system of a set pension for the widow of each rank was and still is wrong. A means test should be applied, since it seems very unfair that a wealthy woman in her own right or one left very well off should be given a full pension when widows with no private means and in a great many cases unable to get out to work to augment the pittance were at the very low set rate. It is something I feel very strongly about, even though I was one of the lucky ones with no ties and able to earn a living in later years.

Another thing that vexed me greatly was the civilians who got 'gongs' when it was their workforce who had done the hard graft. As the largest organisation in CVWW, the Y naturally got more medals to dish out than the others. Of those given out, the only recipient who *really deserved* it was Harry Hunt. He did a stupendous job and was up front all the way, working in ghastly conditions under fire most of the time. Miss Harding got her 'gong' for work done, I believe, in the blitz in Bristol and the third went to a poor stray creature who was so vague that she could not take a message across the road without either losing her way or forgetting what it was. She had come out at the end of the war and was shuffled around from place to place because she was so useless. I asked why she got a gong when there were such marvellous people who had gone home broken in health from the splendid, untiring work they had done.

'Oh, we had to give it to her. Her father's very rich and donated three tea-cars to the Y.'

I could have named a dozen people who had slogged from Normandy working under canvas there and carried on running the most splendidly big outfits in dreadfully adverse conditions. Several of these good souls had nervous breakdowns from sheer exhaustion, both mental and physical. Surely their tirelessness was worth more to the men than three tea-cars, whose cost to 'Daddy' would have been no more than a 'Dinky Toy' to the average person. As I have said, Robbie, who should have got a knighthood for his work, had to wait forty years for his CBE. This is not sour grapes on my part, for I did nothing to merit a gong, nor did I want or expect one. It is only a sense of fair play to those who did merit recognition that makes me speak out.

One 'extramural' activity that was thrust upon me at HQ but was unknown to the powers that be, was acting as a sort of 'Agony Auntie' to various officers, both known and unknown. My stream of visitors did cause a few eyebrows to be raised, especially as I was often unable to introduce them since I did not know their names. Officers are supposed to be self-contained, able to cope with their own worries, but like their ladies and the Miss O'Grady's, they and their men are brothers under the skin and only human.

It all started by Charles Beach of the Pioneer Corps trying to sort out a domestic trouble with a new Second-in-Command he was sent. In desperation, he brought him to the Club one evening and asked me to have a chat with him after dinner. By 2 am, with me feeling the need for a pair of crutches under my eyelids, he had poured out his life story, his hopes and fears for the future and his matrimonial difficulties. I had not uttered more than two words during the whole saga, but he said he felt much better for having told someone. I gave him a stiff glass of schnapps and sped him on his way to Badlippspringer.

What troubled these men most was being out of touch with their wives: this applied in nearly every case to the war-time officers, since the regulars and their wives were more attuned to Army life and had a better mutual understanding of separation and loyalty. I did my best to explain to them that though their cosy image of going up on the 8.10, home on the 5.15, slippers and pipe by the fire in the winter, pottering in the garden in the summer, with all the local lads in the pub on Saturday had been sadly disrupted, they had found new friends, interests and loyalties, becoming temporary bachelors again. And their wives, unshackled themselves from being 'good wives and mothers' who never went it alone anywhere, had perforce to take on some form of war work where they too had made new friends, with different interests, and were becoming persons in their own right, making their own decisions. This therapy seemed to work, because they went away with a smile. Sometimes they would write to thank me, telling me that all was well. On the other hand, if both partners had been having a 'whirl' with either a GI, a nurse or any handy female, they were told about people in glass houses.

When telling Vandy about my 'Citizens' Advice Bureau', I ended by saying that after giving the poor wretches these 'pearls of wisdom', I always felt as if I was coming out of the judging ring wondering if I had made the right choice and put up the right horse, or made a first-class mess. How he laughed, saying, 'It sounds as if you were cut out to be a Bishop's wife!' It was all very sad, and naughty of me to laugh at the poor chaps.

Robbie got the bright idea of bringing Harry Hunt into the Mess to help me. It was heaven to work with him; he was so understanding and good with staff. Frau Wember, our cook, was a magician with the rations. But the conservative English were difficult in the extreme about anything but bangers-and-mash, plain roast or boiled. Frau Wember, Harry and I connived at camouflaging some of the more simple vegetables which we, armed with our little packets of coffee, cigarettes and sugar, used to bring back from our foraging expeditions (Frau Wember instructing us as to where the best of whatever vegetable we wanted was grown). Kohl rabi we put on the menu as spring turnip, and salsify as young parsnip in white sauce, (what sacrilege!). Spinach beet was a wonderful prop, giving three vegetables – the green leaf, the stalk and the beet – for the price of one. The centre stalks of the leaves, tied in bundles and served with melted butter were an excellent substitute for seakale – but would they eat seakale! However, gradually they timorously tasted these lovely fresh vegetables, deciding they were not poison.

Two Polish secretaries whom I used to meet walking in the early hours of the morning when I was riding Erna in the woods, brought in all sorts of delicious fungi. One girl had been a student of botany before she was put into Buchenwald, and she taught me the right mushrooms to pick. Frau Wember verified that they were safe and served them up with our bacon for breakfast. All went well until one of the staff looked out of her window and saw these girls with their very colourful baskets of 'toadstools' – Harry and I were then on the carpet for trying to poison the mess. We politely pointed out that everyone had been eating the 'toadstools' for the last ten days with no ill effects. It was an ill wind, however, for with the more timorous rejecting the fungi, there were more for the sensible ones, the rest going, well camouflaged, into delicious stews and pies.

We often used to take Frau Wember with us on our expeditions because she did not approve of our standards of shopping – we did not get the vegetables in their prime. She showed us the big *schloss* where she and all her family had worked on the estate. The old Baron and all his family had been shot and it had been taken over as one of Hitler's human stud farms where selected beautiful pure Aryan girls were sent to breed with pure Aryan males. It was a fine old estate, surrounded by high walls with beautiful and massive wrought-iron entrance gates. It turned out that the professor's SS man was one of the 'stallions'; he was supposed to be a 'superman' in physique. Shortly afterwards he was picked up and stood trial for several atrocities at Nuremberg. Coco, who had been brought up on his father's stud farm in Lens, had been the best child rider in Belgium before the war and was now coming on as a very good amateur race rider, used to say that 'Old Whiskers' – his name for the professor – had a good eye for a colt!

At this time one of the Polish secretaries fell ill with a bad sore throat, but refused to have a doctor. Joanna, our own doctor for the little enclave, was most kind and gentle with her, and eventually we persuaded her to let herself be examined. She would only allow this, however, if I stood beside her and held her hands. Toughened as we were by what we had seen, we were nearly sick when we saw the poor girl's body: she had been savagely mutilated. One breast had been hacked off without anaesthetic, then cauterised with a red-hot iron bar. She told us they used to heat these bars red-hot and beat the girls with them. Her whole body was a mass of burn scars and the lower part of her anus had been burned away by the insertion of one of these irons. How she functioned normally was a miracle due to the skill of an American surgeon. The other girl had had all her finger- and toe-nails pulled out and then her toes chopped off with a red-hot, axe-like instrument. Three of her fingers were also missing. This was all done in Buchenwald's medical experimental torture rooms.

Buchenwald was by now a service sports and rest centre. Harry and I took a poor USA Y padre there for a rest. We saw the museum, which was grizzly in the extreme. The officer in charge offered me a beautifully made saddle of the Stübben type, completely mounted. I asked why I was singled out for it – 'Because no one else wants it.' It was, I discovered, made completely of human hide – needless to say, on that discovery, I returned it when we went down to collect the padre. Although some people kept the lampshades and other human artefacts as souvenirs, I could not do so.

I had by now already done more than my stint, so it was soon afterwards that, like the Arabs, I folded my tents and stole away, choosing to do so when Bill Laing was away. Robbie and one or two of my Army pals gave me dinner at the Club, and when we got home I was very touched by the fact that Frau Wember had baked and iced a beautiful cake for me. The whole civilian staff trouped into the sitting-room in our own house carrying cake, glasses and a bottle of champagne. They all curtsied deeply and wished me god speed and a happy future.

— 9 —

# ERNA GETS AWAY

For the four months I was in Bad Salzuflen, Bob Roberts and the Town Major had fixed Erna up in an excellent billet with one Herr Heindrik, a nice old farmer who bred Trakenen horses and Bavarian oxen. He had been a prisoner of war in the UK in 1915.

Herr Heindrik's pipes intrigued me with their *speichel quast* (the spittle-collecting tassels hanging from German pipes). He used a different pipe every day, some of them most beautifully carved. When I got to know him better, he used to ask me into his large kitchen, which was a collector's paradise like the baronial hall of the *schloss*. The walls were covered with pipe-racks: he had the most marvellous collection from an old English Clay and Church Wardens to genuine opium pipes. The carvings on them ranged from the beautiful to the crude and obscene, some of the latter so cleverly done that you had to look twice before the real object in the carving emerged. He told me he had started collecting them when he was a boy and had once got a beating from his father, who had sent him to a sale to buy an ox, when he returned with an English saddle and a boot box full of pipes. As a POW in Yorkshire in the First World War, he continued his collection. If it is still intact it must be worth a king's ransom.

His wife was large and jolly as well as being a relation of our own cook, Frau Wember. He was small and square, with a weatherbeaten face and twinkly blue eyes. With his (what I called) deep-sea Herrin Volks cap, all that was needed was a fisherman's jersey and a gold ring in his ear and he would have been a dead ringer for any of the Severn fishermen who lived at Saul or Frampton. He had worked on a stud farm in Yorkshire. He told me he was well treated and very happy there. At first his English was rusty but after a few weeks it came back to him. He and Erna were very good friends.

93

He charged 3 Reichsmarks (7/6d then; 35p now) a week for her stable, litter, hay and grazing which she shared with his beautiful oxen. Her shoes he greatly admired, as did a very old blacksmith who dressed his young horses' feet. John Hall had sent out more nails and a spare set of shoes, so getting her re-shod now was no problem. I worked the same pattern principle for his big Trakener stallion, whom he used to let me or Coco Bertouille ride.

I had now had Erna for about nine months and her wounds were well healed, but owing to her 'tender years' I did not do more than lightly hack her for about three-quarters of an hour in the early morning: it was my safety valve to get into the fresh air and the woods of Berg Kirken, away from the constant bickering and in-fighting at HQ. I had my own hunting saddle, fully mounted, a new egg-butt snaffle bridle which Hayes of Cirencester sent out to me, plus a set of brushes. Now nicely trimmed up and lightly groomed, Erna was every inch the working model of what a high-class small hunter should be. She had from the slow exercise built up more muscle than the average two-year-old and despite her typical Han-overian/Araby looking front walked on really well. When riding out I wore my khaki beret with the Y badge on it and my nicely cut Barathea battledress top with riding breeches and field boots. The *tout ensemble* looked well, keeping the British flag flying.

To get to the woods we had to go through the main part of the little town outside the barrier which blocked off the natives from the CVWW's enclave and other paramilitary departments. Coming back one morning at about 7 am, a staff car pulled up, out of which emerged a scruffy, unshaven half-Colonel. He looked as if he had slept in his uniform (I discovered on further unwanted acquaintance that personal hygiene or dapper appearance were *not* his forte). Without saluting or preamble, he barked: 'Who owns that quad?'

I said, 'I do.'

Silence for a minute, then in his Kentish twang: 'Where did you get all the tack?'

'I had it sent out by my saddler.' He eyed my shoulder rank stripes and four war ribbons; on my sleeve I had under CVWW and YMCA the badges of the units I had served with.

'Quite the little campaigner, aren't we?' Then picking up a foreleg, he looked at Erna's shoes and asked 'Who shoes her?'

'A blacksmith.'

'Don't give me that insolence. Where did you get the shoes from?'

'From my blacksmith in England.'

He then mimicked an upper-crust accent: 'My saddler, my blacksmith, my quad: well, you don't bloody well own the whole bloody Army. You won't have that quad for long as I need her in the Army riding school. You can let that tack go with her as we need that too.'

Speechless with rage, I kicked Erna into a trot and left him, having noted his rank and regiment.

He was, with no disrespect to many of them, what would have been termed a 'Ranker' in the First World War (a man commissioned on the field from the 'ranks'). About a week later one of the maids ushered the Town Major, Herr Heindrik, a Bombadier and a Lance Corporal into my office. The former two gentlemen were in a rage, the two latter distinctly scared.

Herr Heindrik had been having a quiet smoke when the Bombadier and his coadjutor burst into his kitchen demanding Erna, her tack and her trailer: the latter they had already hitched up to their jeep from where it was parked in the yard. They waved a document of requisition under his nose, saying it was their CO's orders. He kept his cool, as they say, and asked them to go with him. As a civilian, Herr Heindrik could not get to me through the barrier without a pass. He carted the two NCOs off to the Town Major, knowing all was not above board, for only that morning he and I had discussed when he could get the blacksmith to attend to Erna's shoes.

The Town Major, who was a pal of mine, stuffed the lot of them into his staff car and steamed up to me. Naturally he asked if I had given consent for Erna to go. As I assured him I had *not*, and informed him of the early morning episode and what the 'gallant' Lt. Colonel had said, he blew his top at the two NCOs and threatened them with arrest for misappropriation of civilian properties and unauthorised entry into a man's premises, etc. He sent them back with his driver to Herr Heindrik's, telling him to collect a Red Cap on the way to ensure that they did not take the trailer or anything else from the yard. He then assured me that under no circumstances could the 'gallant Colonel' requisition Erna. She was mine and mine alone, had all her papers (albeit slightly incorrect) to prove it, and was stabled at Herr Heindrik's on his orders and came under his jurisdiction – a slight bluff.

For several weeks Erna and I enjoyed our amble in the woods

every morning. Herr Heindrik's cow men used to take her with the oxen to her pasture about a mile away over a level crossing, but I liked to bring her in in the afternoon as it gave me another break between tea and dinner. To do this I used to lead her from the jeep, travelling in first gear. She was completely tank, traffic, bomb and train proof, having lived for the last six months amongst the vehicles of war. If you caught the level crossing, like traffic lights, right there was no delay, but if one of the huge, never-ending rehabilitation trains was going through you could be marooned for the best part of twenty minutes. These trains had huge American-type engines which emitted fearsome shrieks worse than any banshee. The cattle trucks were over-stuffed with humanity, and the singing, shouting, jeering and catcalling of the overflow sitting on their roofs all added to the cacophony. Erna showed a mild interest as the first few wagons trundled by, then becoming bored showed more interest in foraging round inside the jeep in the hope of a ginger biscuit or a pear, apple or anything that might allay her boredom and her gnawing pangs of hunger until she got back to her stable for her evening feed.

Our old CO, Colonel Mumford, would often come up for the weekend and bring one or two of what he called his 'new boys': one was a hunting man called 'Jack' who naturally was interested in Erna. Jack was filled with admiration at Erna's stoicism in the face of an extra-long train. At the home side of the crossing was a lane leading to another farm. As we were getting up a little speed, with Erna going into a hound jog, the farmer elected to take his flock of sheep to another field across the road behind us. During all her twenty-eight years, sheep and water were Erna's two *bêtes noires*. Colonel Mumford was sitting in the back of the jeep holding her leading rein. The sheep as usual were bleating at being driven. Hearing the unaccustomed noise, Erna looked round. The horror of the bawling, bobbing, woolly things coming up behind her was too much for any right-minded filly to take: she plunged sideways to avoid the jeep, which she passed full gallop, having tweaked poor little Colonel Mumford out onto his backside on the road. Jack was all for me going after Erna, as he said judging by the Colonel's language he was OK, but I knew she would come to no harm with her mind on the grub stakes. When we had reinstated the Colonel and all stopped laughing, we asked him if he had been hurt. He

The author with Robin
Ashorne Goodfellow in
Gloucester Terrace,
London, the day before
war was declared.

Members of 18 Company
Pioneers Corps at
Tessenderloo in
November 1944.
From left to right:
(top) Lt. Charles Blagg,
Lt. Asquith,
Captain Roy Davis;
(bottom) Major Askew,
Major Willis,
Lt. Eric Furze.

*Above left*
Captain Frank Conway-Upton,
Adjutant of 27 CRASC,
the author's unit
throughout her wartime
service with the Y.

*Above right*
Major Charles Beach of
71 Pioneer Company.

*Right*
Colonel Fritz Renton,
Pioneer Corps Commander.

*Above left* Lt. Colonel Roy Mumford ('Tiger Tim' or TT) of 27 CRASC.

*Above right* The original Old One-Two sign which hung above TT's chair in his office.

*Below* 27 CRASC at Freistett in 1945 giving the Old One-Two sign. From left to right: Captain Iles QM, Padre Saunders, Lt. Maurice Thornton, Captain Frank Conway-Upton, the Analyst Major Ernest Hopkins, the Second-in-Command Major Dick Lewis and Lt. Colonel Roy Mumford.

*Above* The famous three-hare
window at Paderborn.

Hermione Wolf (now Mrs Laurence Waller),
of the WVS, with whom the author worked
at Minden after the war.

*Opposite top*
The author in 1949.

*Opposite lower left*
The author's cousin, Vanessa,
in Helsinki in 1950 about to
walk to Lapland.

*Opposite lower right*
A rather different image
of Vanessa – giving a press
conference on her return
from Lapland.

An oak leaf – with two wolves worked into it – from the famous tree in Guernica where the two wolves appear when there is going to be a disaster.

At a charity ball for sailors in 1962 while working as an appeals secretary. From left to right: Captain C. E. Twiston Davies, the author, Lady Guise, Mrs Twiston Davies and Captain (now Sir) John Guise.

Erna at the age of 22 in the field at Stonehouse, Gloucestershire, with some of her 'followers'. The dip in her neck from her war wound is still obvious.

Erna at Stonehouse aged 24, with the author and her three bull terriers.

The author in 1969
with Scali Rua,
Erna's great friend.

The author in 1982
with Miss Rafferty,
daughter of her
foundation mare.

said, no, only his feelings – that he never had liked mutton or horses!

For a while all was quiet on the Erna front. During August the Army were buying black horses as remounts for the Guards, sending them home when they had collected a trainload. With these horse trains, a certain number of privately owned horses were allowed to travel provided their owners paid expenses, which were minimal, had them Maleine tested for glanders and got a permit from the Ministry of Agriculture and Fisheries. Erna and two other horses, the property of fairly senior officers, were ready to go on the next horse train, their tests and papers all in order.

Montgomery had with him the little grey Arab he had captured from Rommel in the desert and now used to peacock about with in Germany for self-propaganda. This he sent home with the previous horse train to the one our three horses were to go on. A week later he put it in orders that *no* privately owned horses would be accepted on these trains, nor would any officer's privately owned charger be permitted to leave BAOR. This was a typical 'Monty' action which did nothing for his popularity amongst the hierarchy who knew that when he got what he wanted the rest of his officers could go hang.

When my old CO in East Anglia was schooling me for Army Welfare, he drilled into me two rules. One, you can get away with anything in the Army if you are not found out; two, all red tape can be unravelled by finding the right end by which to pull it. The other two officers, like me, were genuinely fond of their horses, being due for demobilisation in a short time and not relishing the thought of having to leave them in BAOR. Not wishing to name names, I still had a good deal of 'clout' in high places, which I now used but, like Brer Rabbit and the Tar Baby, I lay low and kept quiet about it. My friends put their exalted heads together, coming up with the answer that as I was only a camouflaged civilian and was now working for the Y only and not under military jurisdiction, they could get me a permit to take Erna out of BAOR, *but* I was to keep quiet about it: sadly, they could do nothing for the other two horses.

After Monty's edict had gone forth, the 'gallant Colonel X' saw his chance. He went underground to get Erna, calling on our Big Chief Bill Laing with a bluff that no privately owned horses could be kept in civilian billets from now on. Laing was away: it was Bob Roberts whom he met – and was rightly kicked out of his office. But he was not letting up.

My cousin Vanessa, who was very tall, had just done the long haul in her stores truck from Brussels and was relaxing with a drink and cigar (we both smoked them as they were so cheap and good) on my balcony. Frau Wember was going through the next day's menus and numbers with me. It was our afternoon get-together time about our domestic and catering affairs when we were fairly free of interruption.

Suddenly the door of my office burst open, admitting the 'gallant Colonel', who was still smarting from being sent about his business by Bob. Without any preamble he shouted: 'Now look here, m'girl' – he was a little set back at being told I was *not* his girl, was rather busy and that it was customary for officers and gentlemen to knock before entering a private office. Frau Wember I engaged in an unnecessarily lengthy dicussion about vegetables. Vanessa he never noticed. When Frau Wember curtsied and withdrew, he came up to my chair and put his arm around my shoulders, saying in a fatherly way, 'Now, my dear, you must be sensible: you will never ever be able to take that filly home with you. She and her tack will be safe with me in the school and you can come over and ride her whenever you like.' Then, with what was meant to be a knowing, ingratiating smile, he put one of his dirty fingers under my chin (by this time I was nearly sick from the smell of his BO), and tightening his grip on my shoulders he pushed his greasy face into mine, saying, 'You could ride her in the evening session; then we could have a nice little dinner and who knows what might happen after that? Hmmm?' The last 'm' of the 'Hmmm' had not left his lips when I hit him a stinging slap on the face that set him back on his heels. Losing his temper completely, he picked me up off the chair by my epaulettes, shaking me like a rag doll and shouting that I was a little hellcat whore and would pay for what I had done. Vanessa, who was enjoying all this hugely, stepped into the room through the French doors, glass in one hand, cigar in the other and barked, 'Put my cousin down *at once*. I will send a report forward about your conduct as unbecoming to that of an officer.' Seeing this tall officer against the light, he dropped me like a hot brick and bolted. I sat down and laughed because it reminded me so much of my Lady Mother when a foxhound pup was running off with a shoe. She used to say: 'Drop it *at once*.'

It was not the last time the gallant Colonel was to suffer at our hands. Having organised Erna's extradition, I had then set to work for the other two horses. Both men were rather angry, thinking it was because I was a woman that I had got away with it. My late husband was distantly connected through marriage to the Hohen-Lohe Langenburgs, one of whom I knew was a dedicated horse lover, though now a very tired old man. I fixed a meeting and put Plan Two into action. The two officers nominally sold their horses to him, and then in due course he re-sold them to some French friends of theirs. It all took time, with 'Mil Gov' sticking its nose in, but both being thoroughbred mares they stood a better chance than half-breds. Just before I left, the two mares were peacefully grazing in Normandy awaiting shipment to the UK. Their respective owners kept in touch with me until the early 1960s, when they, like our beloved horses, went to their own reward.

Lt. Colonel R. H. Stalker RAVC, aided by his trusty sergeant, got all the papers in order for Erna (the sergeant got a bottle of whisky and two pairs of NAAFI sheets for his trouble). Under the circumstances he ordered me not to tell anyone but Bob Roberts, for whom he had the greatest regard, and the courier who would take her out that she was being moved. It was put about that the next time Coco Bertouille came up from Brussels I was to return with him for a few days' leave and bring back one of our big tea-cars full of stores.

On Wednesday, 26 September 1945, we left the Mess at 6 am, collecting Erna and her trailer, and were on our way by 7 am. Frau Wember had excelled herself in the food basket she had prepared for us. We went like bats out of hell, as fast as roads and the 15 cwt. would permit because we had a premonition that there could be trouble. Once out of Germany no one could touch us. We got through Münster and Burgsteinfurt without incident, had a snack, saw to Erna and headed for the frontier guardpost. In front of us was a convoy of trucks with leave and demob personnel who were taking time for their papers to be sorted. The Orderly Sergeant, seeing the Y badges, also knew Coco, who went through every fortnight or so. He called us to the head of the queue, stamped our passes, wished us well and myself a nice leave. As we left the guardroom, a very agitated lieutenant of the same regiment as the gallant Colonel X dashed up: he was in such a dither than his voice rose in a squeak: 'There is a horse being taken out of BAOR illegally. I've been ordered to stop it!' We walked on to our 15 cwt. to see Erna and it surrounded by Red Caps chatting her up. They were only curious and in no way connected with the lieutenant. Apparently he had been sent off out of the guardroom with a flea in his ear and as we were moving off stood in front of the lorry demanding that the Red Caps take a hand. I showed Erna's pass to them with the three signatures on it. Very politely the sergeant said: 'I fear, Sir, there is nothing we can do about it with this movement order.' The barrier lifted and we were out.

On my return to HQ I discovered that one of the Y secretaries who was 'walking out' with a fellow officer of the gallant Colonel's had somehow got wind of Operation Extradition and had told her boyfriend the night before. He, as a good joke, had told the gallant gent next morning that his eye had been wiped.

It was a long haul; nine hours via Enschede, Arnhem, Nijmegen, Breda, Antwerp and finally Brussels. In Antwerp there was a very good Y, at which we pulled up for a cup of tea, our liquid refreshment having run out. As we were drinking it, a Tommy came in to tell us that the Red Caps had surrounded our vehicle and were trying to drive it and the horsebox away. We tore out like mad things and got them to pull up. We showed our passes and Erna's, so all was well, and we had no further trouble. Apparently these Red Caps were bored with doing nothing and thought it would be a lark to tow the Y 15 cwt. and horse round the corner. At the Dutch/Belgian border Frontier Post the 'gent' in charge who was having a nice little nap, left the barrier up: all traffic was moving back and forth uninterrupted. We arrived at Stokel about 9 pm. Erna had a lovely box in one of Monsieur Bertouille's block of stables on Stokel racecourse. Madame Bertouille gave us a wonderful supper with champagne to celebrate Erna's escape.

Erna was to sail from Antwerp in two days on the *Stork*. After lunch one Monsieur Herfurth of Herfurth & Co., the shipping agents, telephoned to say that Erna's passage would be cancelled as the *Stork* was returning to Harwich with only ballast, with which it was against regulations to take any stock. The Bertouilles came up trumps, offering to keep her on their stud and farm at Lens until she could be shipped. We took her down on the Saturday to where she lived for the next two months with three enormous, comfortable 'pink roan' Brabant working horses, the brood mares and young stock. Monsieur Boul, the Manager, looked after her very well.

After my return to HQ there was a constant stream of demob

parties in the various officers' clubs. It was at one of these that the gallant Colonel X got his final *coup de grâce* over Erna.

We were all pretty 'high' when he appeared, uninvited. He had obviously had more than a few drinks. Coming over to me, he announced, 'Well you bloody little bitch, you got your filly out but I stopped your brass hat pals from taking theirs home.' Stung by his nastiness, I told him he need not worry as they were now grazing on a stud farm in France awaiting shipment to the UK. As a Victorian novelist would have said, his face (normally putty pallid) was suffused with purple. Vanessa picked up a small water jug and tipped it over his head, saying, 'That'll cool you down.'

With us was a Canadian known affectionately to all and sundry as 'Dosie' from his somnolent appearance, which actually masked an excellent brain and ready wit. When the cheers and laughter at the sluicing died down, he said in his slow Canadian drawl: 'By the way, I suppose you will soon be looking for a job in Civvy Street. They tell me the Italians are looking for dog catchers and the pay is quite good. You might do better at that than with horses.' The howls of joy and hoots of merriment that greeted this sped the Colonel on his way out of the bar.

How that poor chap must have hated me. When I saw his death announced in the paper in the late fifties I did feel a bit of remorse because with a warped nature like that he could not have been a happy person, using his bully boy tactics from his insecurity.

Erna's next escapade was a brush with the Customs and Excise Immigration officer at Ostend. By now I had turned my coat into a civilian one so that I could travel with her on the first civilian cross-Channel ship. Coco took us down to the docks in Ostend the night before we were due to sail on 27 November. The first blow was that the Customs official refused us entry on to the dock as the horse had no papers, saying he could not let her be exported. We pointed out she was not of Belgian origin, belonging to a British officer and had her passage booked by the British Consul in Brussels. He was adamant and mulish, like all of his kind: the rules were there and he had to obey them. Where was her entry permit into Belgium? She had none. Coco put it to him that if she had no entry permit, she did not exist so did not need an exit permit. He grunted assent at that but still said she could not sail. We parked her in a military compound and retired to the transit hostel, which had quite a few Canadian officers in it. There was a Canadian troop transport due to sail the next afternoon to the UK. Seeing us looking worried, the padre enquired as to our problem. 'Don't worry,' he said, 'if the Belgians won't let her embark, we'll take her over for you.'

He came with us next morning at 6 am armed with 200 cigarettes which he left ostentatiously sticking out of his tunic pocket. In best Canadian French he informed the Customs official that he had been going to give the cigarettes to him for being so helpful to us, but as nothing could be done his CO was taking the mare on board their ship and thence to the UK.

Within three minutes Erna had her exit permit. She was hoisted on deck by a giant crane and her box lashed securely down. Quite snug with a rug over her and a giant German *oberdecke* or duvet, she was at last homeward bound.

# 10

# BACK TO BLIGHTY

Over the past few months, Vandy had been sending me wonderful letters, colour charts and snaps of the little house and training establishment near Pickering in Yorkshire which was to be our home. He was to meet me with the horse box at Folkestone. The first inkling I got that all was not well was when we docked. On the quay was the horse box, no Vandy, only the diminutive, dapper Martin Walsh, Vandy's driver and batman, very much the Head Lad now, looking more like a bright-eyed Imaal terrier than ever.

Erna, who had travelled in her Jerry water-cart converted trailer, was slung ashore. Martin took her out, walking her about to stretch her legs after the four-hour journey while I wrestled with the Customs. They wanted £50 for Erna and £200 for the trailer, which was all a wicked swindle. They settled for £25 and kept the trailer. Martin gave me a letter from 'the guv'nor': I had to smile – he was the 'guv'nor' now, not the Brigadier. The letter was brief and to the point – 'Welcome home, darling. Confined to barracks by damned quacks. Enclosed for anything you want on the way up. Ring when you've had breakfast.' There were ten fivers in the letter.

We breakfasted at the Majestic, Erna munching her first taste of real rye-grass hay and English oats. Our meal was awful – lumpy porridge, greasy fried bread, sausages with very tired fried potatoes, flabby toast, margarine and golden syrup.

Martin, who had driven through half the night, gladly gave me the wheel, sleeping most of the way until we stopped for lunch. It was wonderful to drive on real roads again but I found the box kept 'wandering' to the right side of the road! A near shave with a London Brick lorry eventually got it into my head that I was now in the UK, where one drove on the left.

We arrived about 6 pm, all three of us travel weary. Erna's first reaction was to lie down and roll in the good clean straw. She had a reception committee of the whole staff, including the 'guv'nor'. We had not seen each other for nearly two years. He was his own cheerful self but so thin. Going grey at the temples, his handsome face on one side looked as if a giant cat had clawed it and he had lost the sight of one eye, but not the eye. I was angry with myself for not coming home sooner. We had a celebration supper and talked well into the night. Then he told me he had to go into hospital in two days' time as there was more shrapnel in his side which was giving a bit of bother and would have to be 'chipped out', as he put it.

He was in hospital for a week, allowed home only on the strict instructions that he took it easy. At the hospital they showed me how to do the dressing. It shocked me to see the hole in his side and the scars down his neck and chest. By Christmas he was pronounced fit and able to ride out again on a quiet hack. He and Erna got on very well together. Not more than 15hh, she was easy to mount and did not pull. Marky Boy, Vandy's old pre-war point-to-pointer/chaser, was still a bit of a lad for all his fifteen years and could clear off with you on the gallops if the humour took him.

We had three horses of Vandy's and three Army friends' horses in training, so the yard was quite busy. It was not very far from his late brother Liam's. Katie, Liam's widow, had re-married a very nice local man, Andrew Johnson, who was also a hunting and racing enthusiast. Our house was usefully convenient, facing on to a gated road with the village two miles away, the nearest neighbour a mile farther up. The stables had been custom-built by a pre-war trainer and there was ten acres of good pasture paddocks at the back. Vandy's great-aunt had left him her house and furniture when she had died before the war. He had kept all the nice pieces, so furnishing was no problem. All was in situ when I arrived.

After Christmas, the doctor passed him fit, so we decided to get married at the end of January. A week before, he took me to his solicitor and made a new will. He had made one in Newmarket leaving me everything, but including a rider that Millicent Jackson, my cousin Jack's wife, was to have an annuity of £500 for life and a home provided either with me or wherever she wished. This was the result of his sick leave, when Cousin Jack had asked him to be executor for his will. Vandy was very shocked at the state of Cousin Jack's finances and the tiny allowance that Millicent would have to live on. Their house, Fairview, was an entailed property of the Kilbees, Jack's first wife's family, so would go to his daughter. Since this will would not be valid after our marriage, Vandy made a new one in which we mutually agreed that Millicent's allowance should be increased to £750 a year. This could not be signed until after the wedding.

A few days later we were out on the gallops. He was again riding his beloved Marky when he bet me that the mare could not jump a tiny wall. She did it beautifully, but to my horror I saw him put Marky at it. There were loose stones on the landing side. Marky landed on one and pecked badly, shooting Vandy, whose Dunkirk-wounded leg had not much grip, over his head. It was one of those silly falls over a tiny thing that so often turn out badly. Vandy sat up grinning, telling Marky he should have known better at his age. But I thought he looked very white. When we got home I whistled in the doctor, who said all was well but that Vandy must not do that sort of thing again for some time. Vandy said I was fussing over nothing.

On Saturday he decided we would go on the Sunday to see a mare he wanted to buy and lunch with some old friends on the way. After dinner he went into the study to do some entries, and when he came back into the drawing-room he said he felt cold as he had no fire on. When he handed me a drink, his fingers touched mine and felt like ice. I ordered him off to bath and bed, saying I would 'go round' the yard by myself. He agreed, saying we would have an early start in the morning. When he got to the top of the stairs, he called down, 'When you're making your tea, put my name in the pot and bring me up a cup.' After the ten o'clock round I made a pot of tea and took it up to his room. He seemed very cheerful but admitted to feeling tired. We talked for some time, and when I kissed him goodnight his face was unnaturally cold. He grinned his old cheerful grin, saying, 'After Thursday there will be no more "goodnights".' As I picked up the tea tray, he caught my hand, saying, 'There is something I want to say to you – oh, no, it can wait until the morning.'

I woke at about midnight with a dreadful foreboding. All was very still. I dashed across the landing but could hear nothing, and there was no reply when I called him. Opening his door, I saw that the bedside light was still on. He was semi sitting up but in a deep coma, his breathing very light.

Dr Metcalf came at once with the ambulance hard after him and we got Vandy into hospital within the hour. I was sitting with him when he turned his head slightly, opened his eyes for a second, and was gone. I like to think he knew I was there. Saying a brief goodbye, I left the ward as if I was poleaxed.

When I got home, I made some tea and took it up to his room, sitting on his empty bed and tried to come to terms with what had happened. All his things I had known in his room at Fairview were there, including the little tortoishell box with the silver inlaid V on it that Cousin Gertie had given him all those years ago for his studs. Opening it, I found the wedding ring that would have been mine on Thursday, and the tiny carved ivory rosary beads I had given him in 1928. He hated cruelty of any shape or form, and disliked all the pictures of the Sacred Heart and crucifixes for that reason: Cousin Gertie was forever chiding him for not having rosary beads, and he told her the reason why. Waiting for the family outside Gill's shop on the quay in Dublin one day, we were looking at these very gruesome pictures and crucifixes: on a stand were some very pretty carved ivory beads which he said he would not mind if there was not the poor tortured figure on the cross. I wanted to give him a birthday present and had just had a good win racing, so later in the day I slipped back to Gill's and bought the beads for 27/6 (£1.37). Asking if I could have a plain cross instead of the one that was on them, the assistant looked at me most oddly, departed into the back of the shop and came out with a plain cross with which he replaced the original. To think that Vandy had kept those little beads all these years.

At home as a child I was never allowed into the drawing-room for tea if there were visitors. Vandy would ferret me out and see that I washed my knees (I wore knee-length boys' stockings and pleated skirts and a jersey in the winter if I was not riding). Soap and water during the day was not one of my priorities, but I did like a bath at night to go to bed feeling clean. Knees, hands and face suitably cleansed, hair brushed he would take me by the hand into the drawing-room, saying, 'Come on, chicken, we'll face the Ephesians together.' When we were in, he would ask Millicent or Gertie, whoever was presiding at the tea table, if there was any tea left for two working boys. It was *double entendre*. In Ireland then a working boy or girl could be any age from 12 to 80-odd. In the poorer farms they sometimes came from orphanages, the girls sleeping in the same bed as the daughters of the house, the boys with the sons. There was a nicely defined class distinction according to the character of the farmer. Some made these slavies, who in fact were as well bred as themselves, eat at the fire on the creepy stool, a tin plate on their knees and a saucerless cup. Others made them eat in the 'back house'. This was a 'lean-to' in which was a rickety table with an enamel washing basin on it, pails of drinking or cooking water, the damp communal towel hanging from a nail on the door, a piece of broken mirror propped in the window, with a shaving brush of pigs' bristles, its handle bound in string, and a half stick of shaving soap balanced on the cross-bar of the never-opened window. There would also be a tin jerry for the 'babbies' as well as a heap of spuds and turnips in the corner. Others, more charitably minded, would allow the slavies to eat at their own table.

When a stranger called who did not know the family and spoke of 'your son or daughter', they were informed: 'Oh no, sir, that was the working girl/boy.' So it was a joke which only the family understood about Vandy's and my position in the household.

Now there would never again be the comfort of his hand in mine or his voice saying that together we would face the Ephesians.

'After Thursday there will be no more "goodnights"' – practically the last words Vandy ever spoke. Certainly now it was so true since his death on that dreadful Saturday night. I had automatically been doing all the routine things one does running a racing stable, as well as the funeral arrangements. Now, sitting beside his coffin as it lay in the chancel of the little Catholic church in which we were to have been married this very day, I felt more than ever like a marionette with a puppeteer working the strings. I listened to the prayers, the Colonel of Vandy's regiment reading the lesson, saw the bearer party form up, the officer in charge making sure that the cushion with Vandy's decorations was secure for the last short journey to the windswept graveyard on the edge of the moor.

As the coffin passed me I laid my hand on it in a brief farewell. No doubt frightened that I was going to get all Vandy's money, Craig and Ailsa, his half-brother and sister, the only surviving relations, looked as if they would like to poison me. Katie and Andrew, staunchly beside me, put me into chief mourner's place, the Colonel following with the others, one on either side of him.

Poor little Martin was unashamedly weeping as we passed his pew. At the graveside the Army chaplain handed me the paten with the earth on it; the bugler sounded the Last Post.

Often I had wondered what thoughts passed through the bereaved mourners' minds at a graveside, if they really took comfort from prayer. As the final notes were blown away over the moor, I was 16 years old and sitting on Brer Rabbit outside Spratstown Cover on a windy March evening. Jack Hartigan was collecting hounds on the last day of the 1931/32 season; Chris Mitchell, the Master, had got into his car with a cheery, 'See you all again next season,' and was gone. As Jack blew the 'going home', a shudder had run through me and I had wanted to burst out crying, but Father's bathroom lecture of many years before kept me in control, as it did now. We had a surprise hunt in the late evening with only the hard liners like ourselves and the Valentine brothers (two old gents who bred cobs) left, Mummy, Vandy, Guy, my childhood boyfriend Brian and myself. 'Goodnight, my lady, goodnight Miss Jackson, goodnight gentlemen,' and Jack was off at that mile-consuming hound jog back to the kennels at Jigginstown.

We turned down the Kilcullen Road. Brian had been promoted to a topper and a red coat, his uncle's cast-offs, that season, and Vandy and Guy were as usual ragging us, and particularly Brian, about his hat, saying that he should save up and buy one to fit him next year, since with the angle it sat on his head, he 'looked like a stage-door-Johnny waiting for some girl out of the back row of the chorus'. Pinching my knee so hard that I nearly yelped, Brian grinned, saying, 'Certainly not, it will be the female lead. Anyway, I'll have plenty of reading material while waiting with all the newspapers that are padding it.'

We turned left for Brannockstown at the top of Kilcullen hill, Brian trotting on through the town for Halvertstown. Mummy rated the boys for the unmerciful way 'you rag those two children', to be greeted with the mutual reply: 'It's good for them. All puppies should have a few fleas to stop them thinking about being puppies all the time.' At the Junction Road that ran up by Giltown and the Hundred Acres, Guy got off his horse, took the elastic on his mother's habit off her boot, holding out his hand to her as she jumped down. Girths loosed, mother and son said goodnight and walked the half mile to their home.

Vandy and I turned up the straight road to Gormanstown. All

this time I was feeling that something dreadful was going to happen. We pulled up to walk about a mile further on. Vandy, smiling down at me, said, 'Cheer up, chicken, it's not the end of the world. We'll have Punchestown in three weeks, then Fairy House and after that you and Brian will be "rigging" the gymkhanas, terrorising the tennis tournaments, then the cubbing will be starting. Here, have a swig of this,' handing me his long saddle flask of cherry brandy. 'You'll feel better when Jesse has eaten your poached egg and spinach and you can get stuck into the scones and honey.' (He was the only member of the household who knew I passed the hated stuff under the tea table to Jesse, Cousin Jack's collie. It was supposed to be nutritious as well as packed with iron for my anaemia). All the time he was talking I felt I was shut in a room trying to see the bright sunny pictures he was painting through black panes of glass. Try as I might, the black glass was there and no sunshine. Brian was killed the following week while schooling a horse for Punchestown.

The puppeteer was at work again, I was handing the paten to the chaplain, the grave-diggers were standing back discreetly. As the Rosary was recited, 'Hail Mary, full of grace: pray for us now and at the hour of our death,' I said the response mechanically. The other Protestants were silent. From childhood I had heard the Rosary, from the maids in our kitchen before going to bed, passing the open half-door of a cottage coming back from tennis or fishing, the family kneeling on the earth floor, the men of the house kneeling on one knee on their caps. I wanted to shriek: '*No*, she is *not* full of grace, and why should we hail her and her son who could allow such dreadful things like war with all the suffering it entailed.' As I stood looking down at the long, narrow box that held all the mortal remains of a man who had been my friend, companion, rod and staff all through the years, I heard all their voices crystal clear, the three young men so good to look at in their red coats, Mummy elegant in her tall hat and side-saddle habit, laughing with us. Now they were all gone. The husband whom I worshipped above all people had no known grave in North Africa; Brian, my childhood sweetheart lay in the family vault in Old Kilcullen's neglected graveyard; Mummy somewhere in the dust and ashes of her bombed home; darling Vandy to be left lying in this ill-kept little cemetery.

The bearer party formed up to move off; the cushion with Vandy's medals was handed to Martin. The puppeteer worked the strings to make the marionette say and do the correct things. I could not bear to see the earth being shovelled on to the coffin. Bowing towards the grave, I turned abruptly away. Reaching the cemetery gate, I turned and made what must have looked like a frivolous gesture: I blew a kiss in the direction of the grave. If Vandy's spirit was around, he knew what it meant. As a small child when I had such dreadful nightmares, either he or Cousin Millicent had invented the idea: after they had calmed me down and were leaving my room, they would turn at the door and blow me a kiss, saying, 'When the kiss reaches you it will tickle you, then you'll go to sleep laughing.' Somehow we had resurrected the habit when Vandy was in hospital. Every night at the door on leaving him, I would go through the old routine.

As I walked out on to the road, I left behind my youth with any shreds of religion that might have lingered in me after the horrors of war. At 32 I was a hardened cynic who, even though surrounded by kindness and friendship, was completely alone, swearing to myself that never would I give my love to another human being. Kindness, yes, for I had received so much from others, but never love, and I never have.

# 11

# PICKING UP THE PIECES

fter Vandy's funeral, for the third time in four years I tried to gather up the pieces of life. The first thing was to take out the trainer's licence in Martin's name. Women were not granted trainer's licences in those days. Then Elliott, the solicitor, rang asking for the will that Vandy made in Newmarket three years before, as he wanted to take out probate. The new will which was made a week before his death had, of course, been left unsigned until after our marriage. Nowhere could the Newmarket will be found. We checked in every bank, advertised all over the place, to no avail. Enions in Newmarket had a record of it, but that was the nearest we got. I am convinced that I burnt it. One filthy cold, wet day before Christmas I would not let Vandy go out: to occupy himself he said he would spring clean his old trunks and deed boxes, most of which had lain untouched since before the war. Always a meticulous man about business affairs, he sorted through the conglomeration of bygones, making neat piles on the dining-room table, and in this he was helped by Master MacTaggart, our cat. When all was sorted, he asked me to burn the dustbin-full of rubbish, not wanting the stable lads poking about in personal papers. The solicitor could only surmise that the cat had knocked the will into a rubbish pile or the dustbin. Four months after Vandy's death, it seemed certain that his half-brother and sister would be the legal heirs.

Coming in from the gallops one day, a man was waiting for me in the yard. He was a thoroughly nasty type, much disliked by all and sundry, particularly poor Vandy. I loathed his approach, even though he wanted me to take a horse to train. Determined not to ask him into the house, I sent a lad in to Mrs Willis, our housekeeper, for a tray of drinks. He came back empty-handed, saying Mrs Willis would like a word with me. In the kitchen I found her, red-eyed and weeping. 'Oh, milady, they've done the dining-room and drawing-room, both sealed and locked them, they're doing the bedrooms now, so I could not get the drinks. They told me to stay in the kitchen until they are finished and have given me a week's wages in lieu of notice.'

'Who are they?' I asked.

'The Brigadier's brother, his solicitor and that awful scamp of an auctioneer from York.'

Realising what was up, I told her to send Willis down to the local for a bottle of whisky and send it out. Seizing the telephone, I rang Andy and Katie, asking them to come over at once, and then Elliott. His reply was not very reassuring, but he would be over. Going back to the man in the yard, I made the excuse of being held up by my solicitor. The drinks came at last. I was by then badly in need of one. I said I would let him know as soon as I had considered the matter of the horse, and sped him on his way. By then Andy, Katie and Dick Elliot had arrived. Putting them in the picture, we made tracks for the house.

Never do I want to experience the ghastliness of that interview again. The upshot was that I was allowed the use of my bedroom, bathroom and kitchen, to keep all receipts of food purchased and be off the premises at the end of a week. That would give me time to contact the owners, get the horses removed, and settle with the forage merchants. Vandy's old horse, Marky Boy, was to be sent to market next day, also the 'useless chestnut mare', which happened to be my Erna. After a fierce wrangle, they were convinced that she was my own property, but I must pay for her keep from the time of Vandy's death. They tried to claim her tack and rugs, but fortunately I still had Hayes of Cirencester's receipts for them. Andy went to the market next day and bought poor old Marky Boy for £15, taking him and Erna home with them that afternoon. All the men were sacked with a week's notice; they refused to give them any references as they knew nothing about them. Fortunately I could fill that gap. They refused to let any of us into the rooms, which were now sealed. There were a few bits and pieces in the drawing-room that Vandy had given me, but I had no proof except my word, so I never got them. On my writing desk was a large, silver-framed photo of Guy, Vandy and myself taken one Christmas Eve on Thornton Bridge at a meet of the Kildares. Our own and

Mummy's copy had gone in the bombing, so it was the only one left. Katie had the bright idea that she would ask for it. Grudgingly they agreed to let her have it. As she put out her hand for it, Craig snatched it back to tear the photo out of the frame, handing her the naked photograph. Even his solicitor was taken aback at such a mean act. They then checked my own personal room and belongings, remarking that when I left next week they would ensure nothing else went out in my luggage.

Naturally this charming behaviour got around and all the countryside came to see me and offer help. Shattered, deadly tired after the war, and all it had done for me, neither possessions nor money worried me. The wealth they got did neither Craig nor Ailsa any good: they were both dead within two years. Andy and Katie insisted I stay with them, wanting me very much to have a flat in their house and use half the yard for training. All the boys and Martin had volunteered to work for me if I would continue. But with such a small capital and only three patrons, horses, wages and forage bills to find, it would have been sheer lunacy, only causing more strain. Lots of friends offered me jobs, living with them as a family. 'You'd be such a help, my dear,' kindly meant but not my idea. Between the wars I had seen too many officers' widows in similar situations. All would be well for a month or so, then the lady of the house would come in a dreadful state and say Mrs So-and-so was bringing a friend to the lunch or dinner party which would make thirteen at table, would dear, kind, understanding Elizabeth mind just this once having her meal in the schoolroom? From then on it would be the schoolroom. The next move would be to get her out of her comfortable bedroom on the first landing and within a year she would be a faceless dogsbody drudge, often snapped at as stupid or referred to as 'that poor old idiot' to the friends – 'I feel so sorry for her, otherwise I'd tell her to go.' This second-class existence was not for me. Having always been my own woman, if a rebellious one, when in trouble I was like a wild animal, preferring to go away quietly to lick my own wounds.

Just before I had left BAOR, one of our BSD officers came to say goodbye. Before leaving, he told me his father owned several residential hotels in London, and if I ever did want a job he could always get me fixed up as an assistant manageress. There always seemed to be a staff shortage. So, putting my pride in my pocket, I wrote telling him that owing to poor Vandy's death, I now needed a job. Within ten days he had me fixed up in a big residential hotel in Pembridge Square in West London. It was perfectly awful, crawling with poor old dears living on tiny annuities. Rooms with full board ranged from death-trap fire hazards on the top floor at £3 10s (£3.50) a week, to rooms on the first and second floors at £6 10s (£6.50) a week, these latter being occupied by an enormous colony of Jewish refugees who bribed the staff unashamedly to get double rations or any extras they needed. The manageress was a dear, and a lady, with whom I got on very well. Then the storekeeper got drunk and fought with the chef and had to leave. The manageress gave Vanessa the storekeeper's job. All seemed to be going well. Vanessa could live with her mother Bertie, and it made life pleasanter to have her around. But the manageress had a heart attack, from which she died a week later.

Vanessa and I carried the can for a fortnight, after which the most awful little man, with a blonde, fat, chocolate-eating, rather smelly wife, came in as manager. We were *persona non grata* from the word 'go'. He sacked Vanessa out of hand, and told me I would go as soon as I gave him an excuse, because, in his own words, 'You're a plant here by the son of the house, and I'm told you are to stay.' Charming! He did make some effort to get rid of me, sending me out at 4 am to Covent Garden. Little did he realise how much I enjoyed the bustle, cut-and-thrust and repartee. It nonplussed him that the vegetables I got were first quality and at the right price. Then, coming in after my half-day off, I found that all my clothes and suitcases had disappeared from my room. They had been taken to a filthy attic room, with only a sagging bed, no washing facilities, a curtained corner in which to hang my clothes and a cane chair with the seat out. Making no comment, I went straight to the owner, who lived on the premises, asking him to come to the room. He raged at what was done, and I was reinstated, but it did not make for pleasanter relations with His Nibs.

While on switchboard duty, I used to read the *Hotel & Caterer*. In a back number I saw an ad. for an assistant manageress in the now-defunct Princes in Folkestone, which was a seasonal hotel. Ringing the number, I found the vacancy had not been filled: I got an appointment, went down on my day off, and got the job. As I had been paid for the week, I packed my bags, went and told the owner that I could not and would not tolerate the manager's

insolence any more, nor would I bring his smelly wife breakfast in
bed every day, so I was leaving and had another job.

Now, the Princes Hotel in Folkestone was custom-built, light and
airy, and the executive accommodation excellent. The food was
quite good and I earned the princely sum of £6 10s (£6.50) a week,
plus full board and laundry. I had one whole day off a week, and
every third weekend off. Wondering why the so-called owners never
asked for a reference – it was now July and the season was half over
– I discovered that I had had three predecessors that season. The
husband was always half-shot on gin, which he kept nipping from a
hip flask; she was having it off with the handsome Anglo-Italian hall
porter. Chefs came and went in rapid succession, as did dining-
room staff. One of my jobs was to serve in the cocktail bar on the
barmaid's day off. This was most lucrative: with my own water-
filled gin bottle I stayed stone-cold sober, getting the reputation for
a hard head, and cleaning up £5 to £7 a day in drinks paid for by
the unsuspecting customers.

The whole set-up was very odd. Madam, the manageress, was not
the owner. It was a syndicate-owned affair, where the tired business-
men brought their ladies for dirty weekends. They were the post-
war entrepreneur types who had made their wad out of the black
market, judging by their flashy clothes and their mode of speech.
One gent came on three consecutive weekends sporting a different
'wife' each time. Casually thinking he was pushing his luck a bit but
amused at all his antics, I came into the lounge one afternoon to see
one over-made-up, bejewelled lady stuck in the hair of another of
the same ilk. It was a pretty instructive scene both language and
prize-fighting-wise: certainly the Queensberry rules or the King's
English did not come into either lady's curriculum. It was definitely
a case of no holds barred. The first 'wife' had him followed, 'wife'
number two joined forces with her, and 'wife' number three was, as
you might say, getting the rough end of the stick. Two weeks later,
to my horror, I was sub-poenaed to give evidence by the *bona fide*
wife who had never appeared, but the aid of a good Counsel got me
out of it.

Then there were two very old deaf ladies who took afternoon tea
in the lounge every day. Lady Tozier, who was ninety and a bit,
sported a real antique ear trumpet; her pal Mrs Smith, a mere gal of
eighty, had a modern hearing aid attached to a box which was
reminiscent of the original cats-whisker wireless in the days of 'Two-

L-O calling'. It made terrifying shrieks and squeals. Their main, fascinating, topic of conversation, was their mutual bowel disorders, coupled with the scarcity of loo-paper. Lady Tozier was quite taken with me, because she said that since the last manageress had come, there was always a new toilet roll in the lavatories. These remarks were made at the top of her voice and could be heard all over the ground-floor public rooms. She also carried a capacious knitting bag. Vaguely wondering why she knew there were toilet rolls in all the lavatories, I noted that the knitting bag would come in flat before tea, but after tea and a visit to the loo, it bulged. Making a pretext of tripping over it one afternoon, I clumsily picked it up upside down and out shot three toilet rolls. Checking the loos, I discovered no toilet rolls, new or otherwise. Her daughter, with whom she lived, ran a guest house in Bouverie Square, where I presume they came in handy.

Then Mrs Lines' Agency for hotel catering staff refused to send any more chefs, so I was requested to go up to town at the company's expense to talk some sense into 'that stupid woman' and get a chef. The 'stupid woman' was as fed up as the staff she sent down, and told me in no uncertain terms that she would not supply the Princes any more. However, I wangled a rather seedy Frenchman out of her. He too was on his last chance through drink and bad temper, although he was a first-rate chef. She warned me that he would only last the season out if Madam did not keep niggling at him.

All went well until one afternoon when I was in the still room instructing a new maid in the gentle art of preparing afternoon tea – with thin cucumber sandwiches – and the plate man, the mentally defective son of the doctor, was having a cup of tea. He was quite harmless if treated quietly, but if upset or frightened was given to exposing himself – an awfully sad case, as he was such a good-looking and well-built lad. Suddenly the serving door from the kitchen flew open and out shot Madam followed by a hail of serving dishes, with a volley of French invective that I do not think any apache could have beaten. Whipping off his apron and opening his flies, the plate man tore into the dining-room waving his bojangles wildly, shouting, 'That's what she wants.' Pointing with his free hand at Madam, he went on: 'This would do her more good than the hall porter's.' The head waiter in the dining-room collared him, leading him back to the still-room. The maid was having the screaming ab-dabs; I was hard-pressed not to shriek with laughter.

We had no chef that night, the commis-chef and vegetable man having to make do.

It was then the middle of September, and my contract would soon be up. Frank Upton, our old adjutant, heard of a job going in D. H. Evans, a three-month training course in buying for women who had held officer rank. He put me up for it, and I got it. It was back to the £6 10s a week limit but I had to find my own accommodation. This was easy, because Vanessa was on one of her hiking journalistic tours, so I became one of Bertie's pigs, as she called her paying guests, and had Vanessa's room.

D. H. Evans in those days was in the Harrods, Dickins & Jones group. The training was most interesting, seeing round behind the scenes in all three of these shops from garret to cellar, making one realise that for every assistant on the counter, there were at least ten more behind the scenes. We were also given brief histories of all three houses, and their merchandise, after which, with the senior supervisor, we were let loose on the shop floor, virtually what was known in Victorian times as counter-jumpers or shop-walkers. Each supervisor had his or her own code of light flash, as had the store detective. When you saw your flash on the pillar you went to the nearest intercom telephone, or could get the detective if there was trouble. Shoplifting was rampant, especially at sale times, and was very well organised for the bigger things like coats and furs. The nylon stocking sales were an eye-opener for me: all the music-hall jokes about sales and the way the ladies behaved in them came true. The Oxford Street front of the shop would be cordoned off by a long stocking counter. Coupons were still in use, nylon stockings as scarce as hens' teeth. The purchaser entered by the Vere Street corner door and exited by the main Oxford Street door. All available supervisors, men and women, plus the store detective, who was a tall, good-looking ex-policewoman, well versed in self defence, were on duty.

Certainly it is a true saying that 'more people know Tom Fool than Tom Fool knows'. As I stood in line with the other supervisors, in came a female from Dublin whom I had known well since my childhood. She had toted a gun in the Troubles, could drink most men under the table, and spoke her mind forcefully. She had complained, in a well-known Kildare hostelry, to her landlord, who had the reputation of being the meanest man and the biggest snob in the county, that his milk was watered. His reply was that he had

117

reared eight children on it. Quick as a flash she came back with: 'It's your cows' milk I'm complaining about, not your wife's.' That episode was nearly twenty years ago, yet she had changed not one iota, still wearing her brown beret and belted trench coat. A six-footer, she had the advantage over the tangled, swaying mass of fighting women trying to get their quota – I think it was three pairs of nylons. Leaning over them, she grabbed handfuls, stuffing them into the ample bosom of her belted coat. Then she calmly walked up to the cashier with the coupons for the allowed number of nylons. The detective followed her outside, with two men supervisors, and, tapping her on the shoulder, politely asked her to come back with the other unpaid-for nylons. For answer the lady swung her fist, lifting the detective off her feet, with a punch in the jaw that would have done credit to Joe Louis. The two men were shaken off like raindrops. By now two London bobbies were on the scene. At the court hearing, she asked for twenty other offences to be taken into account, and claimed that she was a war widow with a large family to support. To the best of my knowledge she never had any children and her husband was the foreman in an aircraft factory. Little did she realise that one of the supervisors was a fellow countrywoman, but like the Tar Baby, I lay low and said nothing.

The apprentice assistants had to pay a fee to be taken on, £50 I think, and for this several evenings a week they got instruction on how to serve customers, deal with complaints and speak properly. The tutor supervisor asked me to help one evening per week: she said my diction and aspirates were so clear. Like the queen with 'Calais' written on her heart, I will always remember the struggle to get the Cockney kids to enunciate 'How now brown cow' and 'Hannah hitchhiked to Haiti to hack a hibiscus to hang in her hair'. By the time each session was over, it was I who was talking Cockney.

Eventually I landed up in corsets, under the tutelage of the famous and charming Miss Kilby, a legend as a corsetière in her own lifetime, being consulted by manufacturers from all over the world. When a department topped a certain figure in its turnover in a year, it was split. For example, corsets, night attire, vests and knicks came under one heading. Eventually, as the department grew, each was split into its own, so that you had a buyer for nighties, a buyer for corsets, a buyer for underwear. Now Miss Kilby knew she would be over her target the following January and

118

asked me if I would take on brassières. But as usual lack of education was my stumbling block: I knew I would never be able to cope with the figure work. As a junior buyer you had to stand on your own feet, getting no help until you topped the ladder like Miss Kilby or Miss Denning, the lingerie buyer, who had their own secretaries. Also I was suffering dreadfully from my back from the eight hours a day standing, and with mental and physical exhaustion. After talking it over with Miss Kilby, who was one of the kindest and most understanding of women, and with Frank Upton, who had got me the job, we agreed that it was really not my scene. Frank agreed with me that the only life I really knew anything about was horses and the Army. The YMCA were still running canteens at camps for National Servicemen, so Frank came up with the bright idea that I should rejoin the YMCA as a relief worker running canteens for holiday replacements or in case of illness.

This was well paid and all found, entailing little standing, as these canteens now had civilian staff to do all the chores and counter work. Organisation and welfare were the leader's pigeon. So I left D. H. Evans and all the kindly people there, taking with me a greater insight into human nature.

The war had been over for eighteen months. Rationing was still on, everyone was tired and disillusioned by a Labour government. All our high hopes and the euphoria of 'all-pull-together' with a will to win were gone. It was like living in a vacuum. Everyone was on the fiddle and talking of long-term policies which nine times out of ten came to nought. As the serving soldiers were being de-mobbed, National Servicemen were flooding into the recruit training depots.

Before taking up my relief duties, I spent a week in Ireland with Cousin Jack and Millicent. Jack was a very sick old man: Mummy's and Guy's deaths had shaken him terribly, but Vandy's had been the final straw. He never really recovered from it, and died quite suddenly the following September.

# 12

# BACK TO THE Y

The first posting in my new role of Relief Leader was to a big recruit-training camp in the West Country, which also had ATS and PHU units attached. The Y had been run by a Northern Ireland Nonconformist Minister and his wife, both typical of their breed, bigoted to the nth degree and not the best material for such a mixed camp. The YWCA still had a lady to cope with the ATS. The *ménage à trois* was not a happy one. The troops got the backlash of the rows, the canteen was literally deserted: there was never any 'housey-housey', whist drives, dances, concerts, sing-songs or boxing allowed. The atmosphere was about as inviting as a bombed-out church on the Falls Road in a wet month of Sundays.

When the leaders came back from leave, the YW lady left. The camp commandant, Colonel Graham, asked me to take over as Leader, but things were in such a mess that I applied for a senior Y man to help straighten them out. They sent me the famous Grampy Lainson. He was a much-decorated *Times* correspondent in the 14–18 War, and famous for his work in the Y in the last war in North Africa and Italy, known affectionately to all and sundry as Grampy because he was the oldest serving regular Y person on their books at the time. He was terrific fun to work with and as shrewd as a wagon-load of monkeys. Eventually, with a new civilian staff, we got things straightened out. He retired and emigrated to Australia where he died some years later.

Among the three subalterns who did most of the square-bashing with the recruits was a tall, good-looking boy, extremely smart, very polite, most helpful in every way. We became good friends, and he told me he was Matthew Gurney, that he came from Thetford and that his father was a retired Indian Army Colonel. He had been educated at Lancing. In casual conversation about Norfolk, he also said that his sister and he would inherit the manor house and tenant farm. He devoted all his spare time to helping organise things. Owing to its very mixed personnel it was not an easy job. The PHU consisted mostly of older men who had seen active service, being either bomb-happies awaiting re-posting, or marking time for demob. The pretty, flirtatious ATS did not exactly help to unite the two factions. The older men resented the Rookies, the National Service men, and the latter resented being there anyway. Actually it was wonderful for them. I saw them come in slouching, ill-fed and ill-washed and, in six weeks, after their passing-out parade, they were well set-up, smart and brimming with health after the good food, fresh air, discipline and physical exercise. Matthew Gurney's platoon always won the cup: the CO said he was a natural at recruit-training, and had a way with men. I asked him one day why he never went home on a 48-hour or a weekend leave: he said the house in Norfolk was still requisitioned and the house in Surrey was let, as his family were in Kenya.

Erna was now installed at a farm nearby, and I rode her nearly every day between opening hours. Matthew told me he had not ridden since he was a child in India when his father gave up playing polo owing to a leg injury. All these stories, coupled with his knowledge of the Brandon/Thetford area, rang true. He was kind, well-read, keen on the Army, and was, I thought, a nice person. His CO told me he would make the big time in his chosen career. For myself, I was terribly tired mentally and had not got enough capital to start horse-dealing again, and the prospect of having to go home and live on my pension, facing the constant hurtful sniping of the Lady Mother, or dragging from wearisome job to wearisome job, made me vulnerable, or as I now realise, unhinged, for had I been in my right mind I would never have agreed to marry Matthew after knowing him for only nine months.

A few weeks after we were married, the CO's wife asked me to tea. It was there that the first bombshell hit me. She asked me what we were going to do in September. 'Follow the drum like any other Army wife,' was my naive reply. There had been rumours of the camp disbanding.

'But, my dear,' she said, 'Matthew's is only a short service commission and that ends in September.' That evening I asked him about it, and he blazed out in anger at Mrs Graham's being a meddling old bitch, stating that, with his father's influence, he could get into any regiment he chose and telling me in the same

121

breath not to interfere in matters that did not concern me. It was a second shock, because neither Guy nor Vandy had ever behaved or spoken to me like that, or indeed any of my male relatives to their wives. Next afternoon he came back looking white and shaken, saying that the CO wanted to see us together. I was to learn from this experience that he always went deadly white when caught out on any of his misdeeds. He could also get himself out of a nasty spot by making himself sick or running a temperature virtually at the drop of a hat.

Colonel Graham did not mince matters, telling us that as an unqualified married officer Matthew would have certain difficulties getting into a good regiment. We selected three that did not require their officers to have a private income and as he did well in all exams, he sailed through his War Office Selection Board exam, and told me he had put his name down for the Gloucesters, the Warwicks and the Wiltshires. This he did not do, only applying for a very fourth-rate regiment on the south coast well known for the poor quality of its officers. But it was not until he was called on to resign his commission a few years later in Korea that this bit of deceit came out.

Whilst awaiting posting, he was put on indefinite leave. My father asked me to come home and bring Erna and the new son-in-law for a winter's hunting. This hurt me greatly because of Mother's behaviour to Guy, but for Father's sake I agreed to swallow the leek. Before we went to Ireland, Matthew took me to meet his parents for the first time.

By now Matthew had admitted that his parents were not abroad. The house was a poky little semi in Croydon, in which neither front door nor room was ever used, being kept for important 'Kompney'. The visit was a great shock to me: having worked amongst all classes, creeds and colours, I had never been an integral part of the lower echelons of suburbia. We were greeted at the kitchen door by what at first glance I took to be the 'lady wot did' for them. She was a small, beady-eyed woman, curlers in her hair at 4 pm, scuffed bedroom slippers, a dingy pinny, a strong whiff of gin blended with the smoke of the cigarette which dangled from one corner of the cruellist little mouth one is ever likely to see. Her greeting was enthusiastically heart-warming – 'Coo-er, you ain't arf old for our Matty!', with which she turned, shuffling into the over-furnished little dining-room where 'Pa' was having his afternoon nap, and shouted at him 'Wake up, you lazy old bugger, our Matt's back.'

Pa was indeed lazy, but the best of a very bad bunch. He had a rough time of it from the beady-eyed old gin-swiller and two utterly selfish, ruthless offspring. It struck me that he had gone under for peace and quiet. Basically he was honest and was really quite shocked when I told him about the manor house etc. He admitted having never been anything but a sergeant, who had seen service in India in the 14–18 War and had never been out of the UK since. Matthew and his hard-faced bitch of a sister had been evacuated to Norfolk by coincidence to the tenant farm of a namesake, going to the village school, and like all sharp Cockney kids had picked up all the gen on the family in the big house. The idea of the fairy tale of Lancing College I was to discover nearly forty years later. Matthew got a scholarship to the John Ruskin Grammar School which, when it was hit by a bomb, was supposed to move to Lancing College. The College pupils had been evacuated to Shropshire, but the John Ruskin move never took place.

Mealtimes were another revelation. The men of the house were served first, then the daughter, myself last. That was, I later discovered, correct etiquette in that stratum of society, daughters-in-law being counted as no account poor trash. When we had fish, other than that brought in from the 'chipper', Mammy set out all the plates round her and proceeded to pick with her fingers the bones out of each portion, the result being a jumbled mess on each plate. I wanted to giggle; it reminded me of the Lady Mother preparing the dogs' dinners in the scullery. There were no fish knives or forks in the establishment: it threw light on why Matthew would never eat fish other than fillets – the poor chap did not know how to manage it! When we had kippers for breakfast, I took mine, operating on it myself. This sent old gin-sling into a sulky silence when she saw the neatly boned and skinned kipper being eaten. All the puddings were smothered in lumpy yellow custard poured from a big white cracked jug with a broken lip, causing the sticky goo to slither down the outside. This gin-sling overcame by licking her finger and wiping it over and round the broken lip *before* and after pouring. Needless to say I became a total custard abstainer!

With all her shortcomings, she had some excellent qualities. She could and did play the piano very well and grew the most beautiful flowers in the tiny postage-stamp of a soot-laden garden. Her roses

123

were lovely and she taught me a lot about them. Also her dogs and cats were really well cared for. In the evenings, when the second bottle of gin was beginning to make its presence felt, her language was ripe, reverting to the fish trade whence she had come. If tape-recorders had been about then, I would have had a much-sought-after dialect collection for the BBC research department.

Before taking Matthew home to Ireland, I gave him a lesson in the correct use of cutlery, showing him the various types and their uses. I also sent him to dear old Dr Sumption (the organist of Gloucester Cathedral who had taught elocution and singing) for elocution classes to iron out the Cockney twang that crept in occasionally. For in my mind's eye I could both hear and see the Lady Mother making none-too-tactful comments about him. Oddly enough, he was grateful to me for what I was doing for him, realising that he had put up such a black with me that he would have to work hard to re-establish my trust in him. But this he never succeeded in regaining because of his complete inability to tell the truth for any length of time. A brilliant man, with a built-in Walter Mitty complex, he could talk himself into any job and skate through exams, but like a badly bred racehorse who could not stay, he would flatter for the first three furlongs, then begin to fade, and when the bat was dropped on him he would run out after interfering with the other runners. Jobs usually ended with instant dismissal, which he accredited to everyone else, including me, as in his own eyes he was never at fault.

# 13

# IRELAND

While my spouse was getting himself a new regiment and hopefully some sort of home for us, we sailed for Ireland. Travelling was second nature to Erna: given the right fare she could have bought her own ticket. We docked at Penrose Quay, Cork, at 8 am. She had travelled in luxury accommodation on the *New Innisfallen*, which also had stabilisers fitted. My father, who met his brand-new son-in-law for the first time, was far more impressed with the nice chestnut mare. It was the first time for over eight years that I had seen my father, who seemed to have aged but was in good spirits. By the time we had got Erna off the ship and through customs it was getting on for 9.30 am. Again she was to make history for she was the last animal to pay her one shilling cocket tax in Ireland: it was abolished that week. Regrettably, the receipt got lost in our many moves; it would have been quite a historic memento.

My father was worried about a young mare in the city traffic: I allayed his fears, saying that the gay abandon of Irish driving would hold no terrors for her. We saddled her on the quay and I rode her over Brian Boru bridge which was timbered, the old railway lines still on it with its high iron staunchions for the overhead lifting gear plus a double line of traffic. She did not notice she was crossing water. We did a nice hound jog up Parnell Place, my father and spouse bringing up the rear with the luggage. There were no traffic lights and Parnell Bridge, with its plank structure, still swung to let small coasters up into the city. At the Anglesea Street side was a Garda (Irish policeman) on point duty. It was now the busy hour when all the business people were coming into their offices. There were two cars in front of us: when the Garda stopped us to let the Albert Quay traffic come across the bridge or down Union Quay, Erna suddenly realised she was standing over water. The bridge had

always made a slight clunkety noise as you drove across it: the
oncoming traffic could have done this, making it vaguely reminiscent of a Bailey bridge. Erna never threw a buck in her life, but
used to make little cat pounces in moments of stress. These she
started to do on the greasy old timbers and only her Mordox studs
saved her from disaster. She also started to screech. The stupid
Garda looked round, laughed, but still held us up. Erna took one
almighty plunge, diving past the two motors and the Garda's
outstretched arm and shooting through the cross-traffic like a shuttle
through a loom. Going up Anglesea Street, we passed the City Hall,
the morgue and the Corn Market at a rate of knots, finally pulling
up outside the Convent of St Joachim and Anne. By the time the
Garda had gathered his wits and allowed the piled-up stream of
traffic behind him through, we were sedately walking round the
Free Church, heading for Evergreen and the back Douglas road.
She dismissed all the heavy traffic milling round her as 'kid's stuff'.
My father had been scared for her on Anglesea Street, knowing that
its polished surface was death to any horse, no matter how quietly
they walked, unless they had studs. Fortunately, when our blacksmith Stanley Hall had shod her the day before, I had asked him to
put studs in both fore and hind shoes.

When we got home, Ahern, our old groom who heard us coming
down from Castle Treasure, was at the gate to meet us. 'Ah! Miss,
'tis great you're back. The poor Master is in the delights. She's a
"bleddy nate shtamp of a mare", not like them swimmers and
whalers they had for the remounts.' (Swimmers were Australian
horses and whalers Argentinian horses used in the 14–18 War.) All
this was said in one breath: poor old chap, he looked so old and
tired.

I knew from his manner that something was up, then he blurted
out: 'She's a blood mare, you can't lave her out at night in the
winter.'

'I've no intention of doing so.'

'I know Miss, but "herself" says she's to stay out, she's not
having a stable taken up with her. Well, we'll see. Ah sure, you
knows well what herself is like when her mind's made up, y'can't
change it.'

'Herself' was not visible when we got to the yard. Taking Erna's
tack off, I amusedly wondered 'who had eaten who' or what
reception her second son-in-law was getting. I need not have

worried, they both emerged like a pair of pussy cats after a saucer of cream. By now I was sponging Erna's saddle and girth mark. There was no welcome from the Lady Mother for the prodigal's return. She walked round Erna, chewing her lips as of old. Glaring at me, she said: 'She's a mean little flat catcher, her pasterns are too short; must be a very bad ride. Put her in the long paddock. I don't want people looking at her.' The Lady Mother was running true to form. The long paddock, which was down the boreen (lane) at the back of the garden wall, was well fenced by high hedges on all sides. In all the years I had known it, it never had a gate, only three slip rails, being mainly used for cows due to calve, the driving pony or to rough off the hunters at the end of the season. It was, by virtue of its position, completely isolated from all human contact except to see the house cows coming in morning and evening. Poor Erna, who loved human company, would not be very happy there. Also with her gate- and door-opening propensity I did not think the slip rails would create much of a problem for her if she wanted to get out.

Father came down with us to the paddock: it was like old times to be with him and horses again, as I had only seen him a few times on his own during the war. Telling him of Erna's little weakness, he laughed, saying: 'Let her get out, she can't come to any harm. We'll have her near the house before long.' From years of fencing with the Lady Mother's quirks and fancies, he had his own methods of circumnavigating them.

On Saturday, the day after our return, my uncle and his wife were bidden to a shepherd's pie lunch to meet the new son-in-law, who by now was calling the Lady Mother 'Mother' at her invitation, much to my father's and my own amusement. We had tacitly agreed to keep Erna's little episode on the bridge quiet, telling Matthew not to mention it.

Like all hunting families, when a new addition came into the yard, all crowded round to go over it with a toothcomb, trot it out and, if possible, ride it. Erna was no exception. Matthew was very upset at having to take a back seat: as he could not ride very well, he was virtually 'written off' by Father and Uncle. After examination, Erna was saddled and taken into the lawn (the field directly in front of the house) to be ridden before lunch. The verdict was that she was a very good ride, well mannered, but poked her nose a bit, which was understandable given her neck wound. My Aunt, not a

great horsewoman, rode her all this time, Erna behaving impecca-
bly. Then under duress the Lady Mother was enticed to get up on
her; she hunted sidesaddle but hacked astride and was an extremely
good horsewoman with wonderful hands. She and Erna disliked
each other from the start, for after all, Erna had met a very good
cross-section of humanity which to her dying day she sized up more
accurately than many a learned judge.

All went well until they started to canter, then Erna, whipping
round, darted under one of the umbrella-like beech trees, going
round it in ever tighter circles like the tiger in *Little Black Sambo*.
First the Lady Mother's lovely long hair was unleashed by a branch,
at which everyone laughed and called her 'Absolom', then Erna
nearly succeeded in scraping her off against the trunk of the tree.
As I rescued my mare, the Lady Mother got off her, pouring the
vials of her wrath on Uncle for making her ride the ill-mannered
little brute astride. Matthew of course rushed up to enquire if
Mother was all right, for she must have had a nasty fright. He got
his first lash from the Lady Mother's tongue: '*Frightened?* What do
you suppose, young man, I would be frightened of? Don't you
know *ANYTHING* about horses?' Leaving him with his mouth
open and us in hysterics, she stalked off to see if *that girl* had the
lunch ready.

The atmosphere at lunch was well charged with static electricity.
To ease the tension, Uncle gave a humorous and graphic description
of the Parnell Bridge episode: he had had a ringside seat as he was
in his car in Anglesea Street on the way to the office waiting to cross
the bridge (being otherwise engaged, I had had no time to recognise
the car occupants, much less to exchange pleasantries with them).
He ended up by saying he would never see a better imitation of
John Gilpin off the cinema screen. Instead of getting a laugh from
the Lady Mother, he got his head snapped off: '*You* may think it
funny, but I don't. I told her if she came home she was to stay quiet
as the Cork people have enough to say about her and the kind of
woman she was in the war. Now with her wretched little mare she
has to make a disgraceful exhibition of herself in the City itself in
front of *all* those people.'

On the Sunday morning I detected signs that the mechanics of
the slip rails had been investigated; but Father's wiring had held.
He had gone to church, Matthew electing to go with him, to 'show
the flag' as he put it. I busied myself carrying water down to Erna's

paddock. It was the only one which had no water laid on. Ahern had had a directive, which he ignored, not to do 'one hand's turn for that little brute'; he used to sneak down two buckets of water each time he went for or returned the cows after milking. But he had got so old and frail-looking that I decided that I would keep her water tank topped up myself as it was a good 500 yards from the pump to her paddock.

After eleven o'clock Mass, the neighbours arrived, curious to see 'Hitler's Mare' – so much for parking her out of sight. They were all the small farmers and farm labourers I had known in my childhood as strapping young men, now old, grey and bent, some even 'wearing' a stick as it was colloquially known, to help their rheumatic limbs along. Mick Murphy, the oldest and most privileged of them, always called me 'Childy', and said, 'Childy dear, ye've suffered terrible – I hope the little mare will be lucky for ye but I'd say the Mistress won't have much "mass" on her.' (By 'mass', he meant 'liking' or 'good opinion of'.) Sunday passed without further incident.

Some deviation is necessary to explain the following events. As will be gathered, the Lady Mother had somewhat fixed ideas, which were made operational by the dogmas she issued. When my father asked us to come home she followed up our acceptance by a letter which was more in the shape of a code of conduct: 1. You will pay for your board; 2. Sleep in your old nursery (as I may need the spare room for visitors) – she never had any except her poisonous cousins; 3. The mare must live out and everything paid for; 4. None of your friends can be entertained; and finally, do not expect to use the family car for gadding about in. Father knew nothing of these company orders. Needless to say, I did not upset him by telling him.

On the Saturday night I had not been able to sleep and went, as I had done for years in my own house, down to the kitchen to make a cup of tea. *'That girl'*, i.e. the so-called lady help, had reported it. All Hell was let loose, and I was instructed that as I was *not* in my own house now, I was not to do so again. *That girl* had to go to bed early and was very difficult to wake in the morning and would only be disturbed; also I had used the wrong jug of milk in the dairy.

To sleep in my old nursery was no hardship: it faced east over the kitchen garden, got all the early morning sun and there was a lovely view across the valley with a glimpse of the Lee going down to Lough Mahon on the left, Cork Harbour on the right.

Early on the Monday morning the sun woke me as it had in years gone by. Getting out of bed, I sat on the window-seat longing for a cup of tea and admiring the view in that lovely amber haze one gets with September sun. Sitting there, I realised the latest gaffe I had made: instead of Matthew being a shield and bulwark against the Lady Mother's slings and venomous barbs, in the seventy-odd hours I had been home, I had handed her on a plate a craven creature whom she was already manipulating into a chambok with which she could flay and catigate me. She had begun to call me 'Her Ladyship' or 'M'Lady' in the nastiest, hurtful way.

I looked down at the garden, which was her most sacred cow – she was a superb gardener, her garden was regimented, laid out with military precision, the hedges clipped, and with no weed having the temerity to show its tiny head on the garden paths. The end near the house had a large herbaceous border which at all times of year seemed to be a riot of colour. To the left of the gate was the large herb bed, on the right the roses. Two of the squares were devoted to peas, beans, lettuce and various small annual vegetables. The long plot under the north wall, on which grew the masses of Dorothy Perkins and scarlet rambler roses and a fig tree, held the four most sacred calves of the cow: a nursery for the propagation of her exotic flowering shrubs, two coldframes, three rows of seakale and the two asparagus beds. At the lower end of the garden at the far side of the well-clipped and arched dividing hedge lived the more mundane vegetables, their plots divided by box hedges, currants and gooseberries, and on each corner an apple tree like a marker on a barrack square.

The Lady Mother's expertise as a horticulturalist was remarkable: not only did she grow exotic shrubs but also vegetables that normally would never have grown in that soil or climate. The house was never short of green vegetables and the surplus was sold to one Mrs Pinker, the greengrocer on the Grand Parade in Cork. It paid the domestic wages and those of her garden satellite, 'Matty'.

Thinking on these things and on how such an unsympathetic personality could create such beauty, I casually noticed that the double doors in the wall leading to the boreen were ajar. This was not unusual because if the vertical bolt was not properly in its socket in the ground, the horizontal bolt would lever open if pushed from the other side – I had done it myself many times in the past. *Then* something else caught my eye: the very familiar figure of a chestnut mare sound asleep on the asparagus bed, which had been given its autumnal mulch topped with plenty of strawy stable manure. In the sheltered corner between the hedge and the cold frames, it was as inviting as feather tick. Having satisfactorily attended to the slip rails, Erna had obviously strolled up to the garden door. For her money, doors and gates had only one purpose – to be opened. A few pushes and the garden door let her into a gourmet's paradise.

Looking across the room to his bed, I saw that my spouse of four months was sleeping in his usual log-like way: woe betide anyone who tried to wake him before his appointed time. No help would be forthcoming from that direction. Slipping on a coat, shoes in hand, I crept like a felon downstairs. Erna was quite pleased to see me but insisted on a luxury roll before I could get her up. Towing her by her forelock to her paddock, hastily replacing the three rails which had been as neatly laid down as if by human hand, I beat a retreat to the garden, this time ensuring that the vertical bolt was securely in place, and with spade and rake set about repairing – or perhaps more correctly camouflaging – her tracks, hoping that the hot sun might dry the freshly raked soil. I fluffed up the asparagus bed, righted the three seakale boxes, whose lush contents had been bitten to the roots, and picked up Erna's droppings from the path. The sampled cabbage and broccoli nothing short of pulling them up would conceal; the roses were well and truly pruned. Praying that a garden inspection might be delayed until the hoofmarks settled, I got back into bed just in time to hear 'that girl' going downstairs. The Polar Bear was still in his hibernation sleep in his bed across the room.

Father was going to a board meeting later in the morning. At breakfast I asked if I could go with him as there were a few things I wanted (which I did not state, i.e. an electric kettle, tea and a few tins of milk for my nocturnal tea-works and to hell with 'that girl'). Later I was to discover why she could not get up in the mornings, since she spent most of her nights with a variety of young 'gents' in the hay shed – but that was another story.

At my suggestion to go to Cork, the Lady Mother launched an attack. 'And what, may I ask, does Her Ladyship want airing herself round the City for?' It was cut short by her garden satellite (who if orbit had been known then, I would have wished in outer space) appearing at the dining-room window.

'If ya plaze, M'am, there's an animal after been in the garden.'

With the Irish sense of dramatisation, he launched forth: 'The sparrers grass and the say-kale is med pandy mash of, yer roses is destroyed entirely an there's no cabbage or broccole left fit to eat.'

The Sword of Damocles descended on poor Father. 'I told you time out of mind not to put that wretched little Kerry cow in the lawn. You can't keep her in anywhere, you must get rid of her.' Some time previously she had got amongst the flowering shrubs, doing them a lot of no good, so having got a bad name, she was immediately blamed for this misdemeanor. Father said he would see about it and we ought to be leaving.

Our various business done, we met for a drink in the Imperial with my Uncle, where I confessed Erna's guilt. Matthew had offered to stay at home and help 'Mother' to clear up the carnage in the garden. Father and Uncle advised that the cow should take the blame, and all would have been well if Matthew had kept his trap shut. I had missed a pile of droppings in the middle of the curly kale; spotting this and making a 'good boy' of himself, he drew the Lady Mother's attention to it. The storm broke in real earnest at lunch, the upshot being that I had to fork out £15 for loss of produce and was supposed to replace the damaged rose bushes. Father said: 'Nonsense, your mother can give them a severe pruning and then they will be better than ever next year.'

The Lady Mother acidly replied: 'What, may I ask, do you know about roses . . . ?'

After that episode, Erna was 'translated' to the lawn where the gate could be padlocked and peace reigned for another three weeks. She was happy with something to see and human companionship. Matthew had returned to his old unit to await posting, which was a great relief to Father and me because his asinine blabbing added fuel to many smouldering fires which, if left alone, would have gone out.

Erna took to jumping banks like a duck to water: Father and I spent happy hours lunging her on the rope over the little banks on Castle Treasure hill (it had not been cleared and put into tillage then). With Father riding one of his own horses, we did our old school across to Howards Bogs where Cork airport now stands. We hoped that the big banks and drains there would give Erna a fall, to teach her to look after herself, but she was much too clever and in all the nine years I hunted her with as many packs in the British Isles she only fell once and that was when she got caught up in

132

hidden wire on a bank. She was brilliant over any type of country, but like so many Hanoverian-bred horses, could not stay; a fast five-mile hunt was her limit. She also had one peculiarity: her saddle had to be specially stuffed. Whether it was from the wound or not, she turned the saddle to the off-side. It took the late Reg Hayes of Cirencester about four fittings before he got it right. Despite her slightly short pasterns, she was a delightfully comfortable ride, so this peculiarity was an enigma to vets and saddlers alike – she did it even in a side-saddle.

It was now time to clip her trace-high for the cubbing. Father said he would turn the handle of the clipping machine. I had forestalled the Lady Mother by buying a new pair of clipper blades for Erna's use. The old Stewart clipping machine was another of the Lady Mother's sacred cows – no one, *but no one*, was allowed to use it but herself. She did clip most expertly. Her obstacles to our using it came thick and fast: blades were out, the little brute would kick it or Father, and if *she* did damage it, I would replace it with a new machine. We did it one morning when she was out shopping with no ill effects to Father or the machine.

The next battle was that of the boxes. Father stated emphatically that *no* horse on his land would be expected to live out at night when clipped. For days the battle raged, swaying round like the Battle of the Bulge. About half a mile away across the fields from us was a big house with very good empty boxes. Its owner, nicknamed 'Toto' was one of a large and gregarious family who seemed to have married into every family in the province of Munster and beyond. They were kindly people who got endless amusement gossiping in a friendly way with all and sundry about the Lady Mother's growing eccentricities. When the battle was at fever pitch, winking at Father I announced: 'Toto will be delighted to let me have a box. I can also keep my own hay, straw and oats over there. They will all love to show her off to their friends.' I then played my ace: 'Nice thing when they tell people that my mother would not let me have a stable – what will the Cork people say then?'

'Oh very well, she can have the calf house where no one will see her in the yard.' I was rash enough to ask if, when out hunting, Erna and I would have to wear a camouflage net so we could not be seen. 'Don't you answer me back, Miss, I'm going against my principles allowing her into the place at all!'

The calf house was a fairly big, very ancient, decrepit, lean-to-shed against the garden wall in the boreen. Its rusty, galvanised roof was like a colander, its door existed by willpower, the rusty hinges supported by a large colony of woodworm. It was Round One to Erna in the stable stakes. As Father and I knew, the door would only survive a few nights. On the third morning Erna had disappeared, leaving a useful heap of kindling behind her. She was retrieved from between the bays in the hay shed.

There were five loose boxes in the stable block, with only three in use. But No Way would the Lady Mother permit Erna to use one. Father said she could have the calving house known as the 'Black Hole of Calcutta': it had a very tiny window high up at the back, the full-length door had a small slatted grid for ventilation. Round Two to Erna – she was now in the yard proper. The door had two solid bolts which she could not get at, and the calf-house door was to be replaced at my expense. Saying that I would mend it, I was smartly told: '*You* mend it? You couldn't even darn your own socks!'

For three nights Erna suffered her stuffy incarceration; then, feeling enough was enough, she started to bang the door with her forefeet, using the rhythm like tom-toms; a cessation, then another prolonged session of bangs, silence, and so on. This went on for two nights until 'that girl' complained that she could not sleep (her real trouble was that Father or I might go down to Erna, and thereby her nightly earnings would be curtailed – the extraordinary thing was that *all* the neighbours knew about the lady's profession and tax-free earnings except my parents).

*That* did it, the mare would have to go out again as 'that girl' must not be upset. Casually I remarked to Father that I had seen Toto while out exercising: all would be well for Erna to go over that evening; he had got a bed put down for her until I got organised. My King of Trumps took the trick. 'You will do nothing of the sort. She can have the top box.' Round Three with the Lady Mother's *coup de grâce* to Erna in the battle of the boxes.

It was then that the fun with Father started. He would not allow any horse or animal to be locked into a stable. This stemmed from the rebellion or Troubles, when to stop the IRA stealing their horses, people locked them in; then, as reprisals either by the IRA or the Black and Tans, the stables were burned. Horses panic terribly in fire, and are very quickly overcome by smoke, so by the time they could be unlocked there would be no chance of getting them out alive. It became a running battle between Erna and Father to keep her in. He enjoyed it as much as she did, saying, 'Now I've fixed you' with some new contrivance, and he would hide in the tackroom to watch her. After about ten minutes, she would come innocently to the door, scan the yard for spies, then set quietly to work. As he would not use locks, we placed heavy draw bolts down the door out of reach; there were a few bangs in the night but with a couple of mornings' cubbing under her girth she had other things to think about and gave him best. They were always great friends – she would do anything for him – but where the Lady Mother was concerned, she was a solid, immovable mass, except to bare her teeth at her or, if she went into her box, put her ears back, lifting one leg in a threatening position. I never in all the years I knew her saw her do that to anyone else or kick at man or beast.

It was during her season's hunting with the South Unions that Erna acquired a taste for stout. The Irish licensing laws permit one in the country to get a drink at any time of the day between 10 am and 10.30 pm (the cities have their 'holy hour' of closure between 2 and 3 pm when you must be a traveller, i.e. live three or four miles outside the city boundary, to get served during it). The country pub glasses were still made of the thick, heavy, greenish glass with a wide top. The favourite South Union drink was 'Tinkers Blood', a half-pint of stout with a glass of port in it, which warmed and fed you on a cold evening, not dying after a time like spirits do. Outside the tiny pub in Ballyfeard everyone was having the usual post-mortem on the day's events. Putting my own glass on the low windowsill, I went to help the Lady Mother down. Erna, who never liked being held, would never move away from me, and was left to her own devices. Suddenly there was a complete silence amongst the group: all eyes were on Erna, who with tongue extended was giving a pretty good imitation of an ant-eater and was mopping up my Tinker's Blood. Ever after that she demanded her half bottle, drinking her glass down to the last drop by dipping her tongue into it. Even the Lady Mother was known to buy her a drink.

At Christmas when Matthew came home on leave he demanded to be allowed to hunt on St Stephen's Day (Boxing Day). There was always a big meet in Carrigaline with usually over a hundred followers mounted on anything from hearse horses to donkeys and jennets. The first draw was Shanagrague Bog, where such a big field could do no damage to the farmland. It was a long and treacherous bog in which were three notorious bottomless holes covered by lush green weed and grass. We all told Matthew about these, which had in the old days accounted for several horses and men who had sunk before they could be pulled out. Matthew flew into one of his childish rages, saying he knew all about bogs and not to treat him like a child. He was to ride Erna, the quietest horse we could get for him. I rode a very green four-year-old belonging to the Master, the late Austin Love.

Matthew decided he was not, as instructed, going to stay in Indian file on the cattle track. Kicking Erna into a canter, he headed straight for one of these bottomless holes. Feeling her forehand go down, she very wisely swung to the side, decanting her rider, plop, into the green slime. Owing to her impetus, she unfortunately plunged headfirst into the dreaded hole, disappearing to my and everyone else's horror. But like myself she was a survivor: when she surfaced, I called her, and two friends made a chain holding on to me with three stirrup leathers, enabling me to wade neck deep and grab her bridle, turning her head towards the bank. Someone went off to the nearest farmhouse for ropes, but she used me and one of the other people in the chain to gain a foothold: inch by inch we got her out on to the bank. Any other horse would have panicked, but her instinct was to stay near me, and my voice soothed and encouraged her. Both my legs and body were black and blue from her hoofs but it was worth it to save her from such an awful end. The wonderful jockey, who got himself out heaven knows how – no one took any notice of him – sat on the bank nearby blubbering that he was wet and cold. We scraped as much mud as we could off Erna and the saddle. My father, who was extremely angry at such a display of cowardice and ignorance told Matthew to take the mare home and do her up *properly*. That was the first rift between the Lady Mother and Matthew. Excellent horsewoman that she was, the whole episode disgusted her.

As well as being badly bruised, every stitch of my clothes was saturated, and my boots were full of stinking bog mud. I had to take my borrowed horse home first. When I got back to Mount Emla, I found poor Erna with only her bridle taken off, still shivering and caked in slime. There was no sign of the gallant soldier. Cleaning her warmed me, taking out some of my stiffness. Proceeding to the house, I found my spouse in bed with an empty punch glass beside him and two hot-water bottles. He had also used all the hot water for his bath, leaving all his muddy clothes scattered about the bathroom. 'That girl' was flapping round him like a hen with a duckling. Mayhap she saw another client in him – financially she would have been a loser.

Our point-to-point at Ballinrea was always held on St Patrick's Day (no Sunday meetings then) or, if that fell on a Sunday, the ensuing Bank Holiday. Only five miles from the city, it drew an enormous crowd of townsfolk. These swarmed over the course and the run-in to the winning post. They seemed utterly oblivious once the first and second horses had gone by that more were coming in, and tired horses and riders would have difficulty in either pulling up short or dodging the seething mass of humanity. It took all the volunteers that could be mustered with steady horses to keep the course clear. Even at the end of a season's hunting, Irish hunters do not have the beautifully schooled manners of their Leicestershire counterparts, so Erna and I were pressed into service.

Since the war, Ireland had become a tax refuge for the New Rich English, who snapped up all the bigger farm houses with a good bit of land. The husbands took a crash course at some agricultural college and then set about losing their war-gained wealth. They worked on the principal that they would teach the Irish to farm, money being able to buy their way into the nucleus of bridge-playing, hunting gentry that were left.

One such lady was discoursing with the Lady Mother whilst I was having a drink and a sandwich which my aunt had brought me. Both ladies had carrying voices. Mrs Shaw asked: 'Can you tell me who is that gel on that awfully nice little mare? I'd like to buy her for Petronella next season: just what we're looking for for her.'

To our amazement, the Lady Mother's reply was squashing. 'That "gel" is my daughter, Mrs Gurney. The mare is a star performer as well as being beautifully bred. *We* hope to breed from her when her hunting days are over. I can tell you *red gold* would *not* buy her.' This was said with all the haughty arrogance of her Seymour ancestors. Both aunt and niece nearly choked on their drinks. It was, I believe, the nearest I ever came to feeling a warmth and affection for my mother.

After the point-to-point, Erna was roughed off, as Matthew had at last got himself into a regiment, albeit a very fourth-rate one. The Lady Mother refused to let my father keep Erna on grass for me, but very dear, kindly friends, the Stanleys of Ballinametaght, took her for me.

My father took me to the boat in the April of 1949: I never saw him again, for he died suddenly in 1952.

Erna and I were now parted for three years.

# — 14 —

# LIFE WITH THE INFANTRY

Matthew's new CO was a big, pompous man who, with a straw boater and a blue striped apron, would have been an excellent stand-in for a Smithfield porter, even to his accent, but without their wit or repartee. Like his lady, he was completely humourless. She was known to the men and officers as 'horse-face' or 'bird's-nest'. This was so apt it made me laugh, reminding me of a surrealist painting of a horse's bleached skull with a crow's nest on its crown. Her badly touched-up hair looked as if it did not have even a bowing acquaintance with either a brush or a comb.

As Army etiquette demanded, I called on her, leaving the appropriate cards. This got poor Matthew a ticking-off from the CO at my forwardness. A neighbour of ours, whose husband was a staff officer, became friendly with me because her husband's great lifelong friend, the late Brigadier Harry Pyne, was a cousin of my father's. I asked her what I had done wrong. 'Nothing, my dear, she would not know. He's only a war-time leftover.' The other wives were a dreary lot. The baby owners seemed to have their brains, or what did duty for such commodities, joined up by nappy pins and green motions. The childless ones' main objects in life were how much they could fiddle out of their husbands for clothes or to have Mum to stay or to stay with Mum. I asked one of them, if she was so keen on going home, why she bothered to marry. 'You must get married;' she said, 'an officer has a lot of standing.' They were the most unsporting, dreary set of women I had ever met. Poor dears, I was as foreign to them as they were to me. Also it was a completely unsports-minded regiment: the officers' chief sport was beer-swilling and thinking up excuses to tell the wife why they were late for Sunday dinner, i.e. lunch, their focal point of the week.

It had always been instilled into me that the CO's lady and the RSM's wife were the two most important people in a regiment. If

139

they worked together, keeping a motherly eye on their respective groups, i.e. the officers' wives and the OR's wives, it would be a happy regiment. If the wives were happy, the men would be happy. One thing absolutely horrified me, which was the total lack of interest the officers' wives took in their husbands' NCOs' and ORs' wives. They positively treated them as if they were untouchables. One major's wife told me she did not know who her husband's colour sergeant was and most certainly did not want to get involved with, in her words, the rank and file. To tell a woman like that that the rank and file were the backbone of the regiment would have been a complete waste of breath as she would not have had the slightest comprehension what it meant.

I made my own friends outside the camp with people of my own ilk, being looked on as a snob and toffee-nosed – perhaps I was. My neighbour, the General's wife, whom I shall refer to as Mrs W, was laid up one time and asked me if I would do her shopping and collect homemade cakes from Seapoint Tea-rooms. The owner was a personal friend of hers, so if the tea-rooms were closed she told me to go in the side door to the kitchen and call out. I duly called at the kitchen door: a teatowel was flicked out at me with the charming invitation, in a very county voice, to: 'Bugger off, I've no time to gossip.' The owner of the voice who followed the teatowel was an extremely good-looking woman in a pretty floral overall. Poor dear – her face of shocked horror when she saw a complete stranger standing in the doorway laughing her boots off! We still laugh over our initial meeting thirty-seven years ago; her husband John rags us about it, saying it would make a good title for a book on how to make friends and influence people. They have both been wonderful friends all these years.

James Brunger, a major in the Buffs, was attached to the regiment. He was a large, stolid, thoroughly dependable, salt-of-the-earth type, again unsports-minded and quite humourless. His wife, Dolores, was a minute, myopic mouse, who lisped through her little twisted buck teeth. Too vain to wear glasses, she got nasty falls over steps and kerbs. They asked Matthew back to tea on a few occasions. They were of the variety who did not have dinner except midday Sunday, but tea about 6 pm with a pickles and cheese supper about 10 pm. Matthew raved about Dolores's cooking. Finally, Mrs W and I pinned him down to tell us what she gave him that was so wonderful. We were both nearly sick on the spot. Menu

No. 1 was toad-in-the-hole followed by ice cream and hot chocolate sauce; menu No. 2 was eggs and chips followed by ice cream and hot chocolate sauce. Had I given him either of the first courses, he would have thrown them at me. As a Cordon Bleu she excelled herself! The teas became more frequent, until I discovered that James was back with his own regiment for a spell of relief duty.

We had been there about eighteen months when Matthew told me not to bother with dinner as they would be away on a scheme which might not be over till late, and he would rustle up something from the Mess when he got back. About 7 pm James called in anxiously asking how Matthew was. Telling him I had not seen Matthew since 7.30 am and because of his instructions I was not worried, James told me that after lunch Matthew had been vomiting, with violent stomach pains, so he had sent him back to report sick. When he returned to camp he found that Matthew had not done so. Sorting out Matthew's driver, he discovered that when they got to the top of Church Lane, Matthew said he was feeling better and would go straight home. Church Lane was a footpath which ran down from the main road to our road, the other road going up to the camp on which the Brungers' bungalow was situated about fifteen minutes' walk from our cottage.

Within half an hour of James leaving, Matthew charged in, flying upstairs as if the Comanches were after him. On enquiring how he was, I was met with a string of invective that I was always causing trouble for him and to go to hell and leave him alone. Ten days later Matthew was posted. Knowing his trick of making himself sick at will, I realised it was a put-up job. After he was posted, the truth came out. The posting was a good one to a crack infantry regiment, and I hoped the better type of sporting officer might have a good influence on Matthew. Poor James was unlucky. Matthew's new regiment and the Buffs went out to the Far East six months later on the same troop ship. Being a major's wife, Dolores went too. She deployed her spare time writing hurtful letters to me about my wifely duties and how Matthew was missing me, and my selfishness in not coming out with him, and never writing to him. After the third letter I put them all in an envelope plus Matthew's letters, which were replies to mine, and sent them to James. He well knew that a subaltern's wife could not get out except at her own expense and if she had suitable accommodation already waiting. Matthew sent me monthly what he said was the full junior officer's wife's allowance – I did not discover until years later that it was only half of what should have been my just dues.

I got a job as Warden of a Land Army Hostel in a very haunted but lovely manor house in Oxfordshire. The Land Army was then gradually folding its tents. I stayed at Swaycliffe Manor until it was wound up. Meanwhile, through the grapevine Matthew's misdeeds began to trickle back to me. A senior officer told me to get out there and straighten him up, but no way would Matthew let me go out. Then I discovered that the WVS were recruiting for the Far East. As I held a separate passport, which did not include Matthew's address, they could not check on his whereabouts. Had they known he was in Hong Kong, they would never have let me go. So after a so-called training in welfare, which had nothing whatsoever to do with troops, we got our postings. I was sent to BAOR.

On kicking up about this, I was told that within six months I would be sent to the East. The whole face of BAOR had changed. We were only glorified NAAFI girls. They sent me off on relief duties: one was to Paderborn, with the Enniskillens. They were very good to me, gave me horses to ride and invited me to dinners on my off-duty evenings. It was a lovely historic old town, being in medieval days the Maynooth (the Irish ecclesiastical college) of Germany. The famous three-hare window with only three ears amongst the hares, yet each hare having two ears, was the test for the poor ecclesiastical scholars who walked there from their home towns. To prove that they had been there, they had to make a sketch of the window. The town had been very badly bombed: in clearing the rubble of a modern church, they found a complete church directly beneath, dating back to the thirteenth century. The archaeologists were greatly excited. I was allowed to crawl in and see. Everything was practically in situ as if the plague had hit the place and the inhabitants walked out leaving their possessions behind.

The terrain round Paderborn was very flat, acre upon acre of pale, sandy soil. All the tillage was riddled with holes like a colander from a plague of mice. They had done untold damage to the crops. Quite uninhibited, they would pop out and stare at you as your rode by, big, pale, sandy in colour, with Micky Mouse-like ears. The hares, for which the area was famous, were also the same colour but about double the size of our biggest hares. There was an old nobleman who bred Arab horses and owned a pack of rough-haired

Dachschunds with which he used to hunt hare. Being extremely old, he followed them in a cross between a rally trap and a Victorian bath-chair. The driving across the tussocky wasteland was the driving of Jehu. Queen Anne's driving in Windsor Forest after her hounds had nothing on him. He lent me one of his Arabs to ride after the pack. When at fault, the Dachs stood on their hind legs, running as fast as a cock pheasant, givng tongue all the time. Their cry was deeper than a harrier and not as rich as a bloodhound, but they were very game little dogs.

I was posted to Minden, to Miss Wolf. Here I must explain my strong disapproval of allowing the soldiers to call the girls by their Christian names, also to behave familiarly, because if a man has a problem, he is not going to confide in someone his billet-mate is having an affair with. It was also a very unsettling time for the regular soldiers with the original National Servicemen being demobbed and always naturally talking about civvy street and what mugs the regulars were to stay. The welfare-trained WVS ladies did not realise that this needed tactful handling and they would give the unfortunate men the worst advice possible, either to write to their MP or this, that or the other thing, and get out: 'Of course, dear, you've had enough of the Army,' was the attitude, which was very trying and upsetting to a lot of men. Because I voiced these sentiments to a senior lady, I was classified as 'difficult', hence my posting to Minden and Miss Wolf. I was told that Miss Hermione Wolf was a difficult person to get on with and that she would soon tame me. The awesome Miss Wolf and the untameable Mrs Gurney fell on each other's necks. She ran an extremely well-ordered club and both men and officers adored her. There were no lengths to which she would not go to get what she wanted for the men. Whilst she was on leave she spent a lot of time chasing a special record the men wanted. On her return, the other WVS lady said: 'How silly to waste your leave on that.'

Miss Wolf's reply was telling: 'Nothing is wasted if it gives pleasure.'

In 1950 the Korean war broke out and Matthew was sent to Korea, so it was unnecessary for me to purgatrate any longer with the WVS. Hermione was also fed up, so we bought ourselves out, Hermione to take up nursing and become rather famous in that profession, and on her retirement to marry Laurence Waller. The awesome and the untameable are still great friends, thirty-seven years on. It was due entirely to her help and encouragement that the first half of my memoirs got published.

Guy and I had promised ourselves a touring holiday in Spain when the Spanish Civil War ended. Our interest stemmed from Dr Starkey's book *Through Spain with a Violin*, and also Lady Eleanor Smith's writings. The war in Europe ended our plans.

Friends of ours in the British Consulate in Bilbao asked me to spend Christmas of 1950 with them. Then you were allowed to take only £35 plus your air or sea fare out of the country. I decided to walk or hitch there in the autumn, and in the meantime to ease out some extra cash via my Irish bank to my friends. Matthew was still supposed to be fighting in Korea; I vainly hoped that active service might make a man of him.

On my return from Germany, the Ministry of Agriculture got in touch, asking if I would take on the wardenship of their Lend a Hand on the Land camp at Eastern Grey in Wiltshire for the summer. This fitted in with my plans, enabling me to get organised and put a bit in the kitty for my return. These old prisoner-of-war camps which were used were staffed by displaced persons of all nationalities. The campers paid £1 per week per head for board and lodging, brought their own sheets or fleabags and drew blankets from the store. Two three-ton lorries conveyed them to and from work, and anything the farmer paid them was their own. Out of the £1 per week, the warden was allotted fourteen shillings (70p) a head for food. They had to have a big three-course breakfast, a three-course packed lunch (this was laid out by the cook in buffet style, from which they chose what they wanted), a three-course dinner of soup, meat and two veg., and a sweet, and supper of tea, coffee, cocoa or milk with bread and jam or cheese and pickle at 10 pm. The mind boggles at today's prices, but then, with a full camp of 150, it was easy, and with luck one might have a bit in hand for the next week's intake if the next intake was under 100. In September, the rate for the potato pickers was reduced to sixteen shillings (80p) a head. These were very rough types, out for the booze and the women, but the food had to be of the same standard.

The campers on the whole were decent and controllable, but of course grumbled at everything. The only casualties were sinovitis in their wrists from flax-pulling. Flax was the 'in' thing for the farmers to grow then. Ninety per cent of the campers were useless, and irate farmers would ring up abusing me about them, that they were more trouble than they were worth, with which I privately agreed. But at the same time I realised that when they got to the farms, the regular workers who resented them would not tell them anything, nor had the landowners the nous to see that they were told and shown what was wanted of them.

A White Russian boilerman/odd-job man was missing one morning: no one could find him. I looked into one of the boiler-houses and found him out for the count with his head in the furnace, which fortunately he had not yet lit when he had had an epileptic fit. The poor chap spoke very little English, and when I got him to the doctor he said he occasionally got these upsets since he was hit on the back of the head with a rifle butt. The doctor showed me his X-ray plates: the back of his skull looked like a crazy pavement, which accounted for its peculiar flat shape. He had what is known as Fulsom's epilepsy. The doctor said 'no more stoking' as it was too dangerous, and gave me some pills to administer am and pm. He came to my office for them up to the time the camp closed. The powers-that-be ignored my request that he be put on cleaning duties, as we needed an extra cleaner. They moved him to be assistant at the sewerage works a mile and a half from the camp. This meant he would be alone for several hours each day when the charge hand was off duty. When the doctor heard this, he hit the roof. The authorities were positively hurt that it was considered dangerous, but at least we got our extra cleaner.

The second cook was a dear little white-haired Irishman, ex-Army, 100 per cent reliable, keeping kitchen, stores and larder superbly, like a Guards' regiment, and careful not to waste anything. The Polish cook would dump three-quarters of a loaf of bread or half a roast of beef into the pigswill if he was not watched. The wall of my loo bordered the path running from the cookhouse to my private back door. The window was painted out, and the louvre was very high up. Michael, the Irish cook, discovered he could contact me there, and on several occasions the conversation went something like this: 'Are ye there, ma'am? It's Michael. There's so many pints left, and so much bread – what will we order?' With his innate sense of Irish good manners, these remarks were all said with his back to the window as if he was addressing the hedge at the other side of the path. My lady assistant, domestic-science trained, had a running battle with him and the rest of the kitchen staff. Her mania was boiling the dishcloths in a strong-smelling disinfectant and re-arranging all poor Michael's stores and throwing out all the left-overs, although we had huge commercial fridges so everything was perfectly safe and hygienic. When she was told not to interfere in the kitchen (one cook left because of her) she started on about Michael being mad, and that he ought to be put away. She prattled on so about nothing, that I never took any notice of what she said. Then our labour officer, a grand man, came to see me one day asking if I had seen any signs of lunacy in Michael. He had been employed by the Min. of Ag. for several years and always his record was 100 per cent and thought most reliable. We called in my assistant. When I asked her why she made these statements, she cheekily said: 'You took no notice of me so I had to get help about it. For the last three weeks I've heard him about six times talking to the bushes outside the warden's back door, and it's always the same about bread and vegetables.'

'Now, Mr Keeble,' I said, 'see what you planted on me!'

'Yes,' he said, wiping the tears from his eyes, 'I also see why the last warden threatened to shoot her!'

Another displaced person, Gustav, the kitchen porter, from Southern Poland, had a huge belly, wore one equally large trilby hat, a waterproof apron and gumboots. He was idle to the nth degree, lying down every afternoon in his off-duty time, often oversleeping. When I called and banged on the door, his snores would drown anything. There was nothing for it but to go in and shake him awake. He always lay on his back, complete with hat, gumboots and apron, his enormous belly covered by a folded blanket rising and falling with each snore like an immense old-fashioned forge bellows. He spoke no English, but God help you if he was a farthing short in his pay-packet.

# 15

# To Spain

Gorringes October Sale enabled me for under £8 to purchase an aluminium-framed rucksack with lots of packing space, a light fleabag, a folding spirit lamp, inflatable pillow and a very good electric torch. My old army mess-tins and aluminium mug (the latter is still in use to bale out the dogs' soup) and old groundsheet completed my equipment. It was now getting colder, so I opted for men's long woollen stockings and a very old pair of riding breeches, the Y clumper shoes and my oldest British Warm with an Irish flash sewn on it. The breeches could be discarded at the Spanish border, as women were not allowed to wear trousers in Spain then. The outside pockets of the rucksack were filled with half-pounds of Earl Grey tea, with more posted on to my friends in Bilbao. A Scot Adey kilt for warmth and smart wear, a couple of jerseys, a little black dress, a pair of fancy shoes, pyjamas and washing kit, and I was all set for the off on 5 November.

Folkestone was achieved in three hops, but I arrived too late for the boat. I got a kip down with old friends in Sandgate, who drove me in state next day to catch the car ferry to Calais, which was cheaper than the passenger ferry. It was snowing hard in Calais when we docked, and the children on the quayside pelted me with snowballs. Just outside the town I got a hitch from a fish lorry with a very voluble old lady who took me to Etables. She got me a lift to Amiens from a cousin, who handed me over to a garage owner who let me sleep in his office. For supper I cooked the two herrings I had pinched from the fish lorry and drank ice-cold water from the standpipe in the forecourt. I was awakened at six to be told that a *camion* would be passing in half an hour. I washed under the tap, drank strong black tea, finished off a rather weary-looking croissant and was whisked off to Paris.

Vanessa was then living with a rich Englishman who thought he was an artist. He was very well-dressed: his clothes and shoes simply shrieked of Savile Row, and he also shaved every day – most unusual for an artist in Paris. His *atelier* and apartment were spotless and very well kept. Vanessa had fixed me up to sleep on the floor of the *atelier* of a once-famous printer, which was situated on the hill leading to Montmartre and Sacré Coeur. Madame, the printer's widow, ran the business and boy, was she a tartar. Dressed in black from head to toe, even her eyes were hard and black. She laid down the law: I was only to stay two nights and must be away before the workers came in at 8 am. For this hospitality she charged me fifty francs (about £1 then) a night. I must also go to her house for the key, not before 6 pm and not later than 8 pm. Vanessa knew nothing of this extortion, nor the conditions in which I slept.

My artistic education was then taken firmly in hand by Vanessa, telling me, as she had done over the years, that neither Bertie nor I knew the meaning of 'true art'. Her rich Englishman showed me his work, which seemed to be all cone-shaped geometrical drawings with different coloured lines. Somehow I do not think it had anything to do with art, but was a façade. He gave us an excellent lunch, inviting me out to the Moulins Rouge that night. The sad but very clever thing that fascinated me in his studio was a huge glass case approximately four foot by three which contained a full orchestra of stuffed frogs.

The next day Vanessa instructed me to be properly dressed as she was taking me to an internationally famous lady artist's studio. I was to keep my mouth shut and learn the real meaning of international art. We walked down some none-too-clean cellar steps to a dimly lit basement ideally suited for a grisly Dickensian murder. The grille drew back to show the grey-green face of a haggard woman, forty-ish, with mad, burning eyes. Vanessa uttered the password and we were admitted. Everything was green: walls, ceiling, carpets, even the dim lights were green. This was accentuated by the only natural light in the studio coming from the thick green glass on the pavement under which most of it ran. The distrait, grey-haired woman had a green chiffon scarf round her head, gipsy fashion, and another green one floating from her scraggy neck; her robe was flowing green, reminiscent of Isadora Duncan; on her feet were the most beautiful green and gold Morocco-leather Turkish slippers which must have cost the earth.

With all this bottom-of-the-ocean obfuscated greenery, one expected to see sea-creatures appear from the multiplicity of ferns and green plants that crowded the studio. The centrepiece and only seating accommodation was a huge green Turkish divan on which I was informed she slept and made love. I wondered whoever would be brave enough to partner such a weird being but was informed that either sex and often little boys sought the privilege of her embrace. With a magnificently dramatic gesture, she drew the curtain aside from her masterpiece, which had already been sold to America for the fabulous price of £3,000. Never since the horrors of Belsen had I seen such a revolting sight. Christ crucified upside-down, painted in the third dimension; the green slime of putrefaction covered his face and body; the hair was depicted as worms; the eye-sockets blank like those of a sheep's head which the buzzards had picked out. The genital organs were a seething mass of worms. The whole was so extremely cleverly done that one could almost smell the sweet stench of human putrefaction. As a child, Titian's 'The Flaying of Marsyas' had always upset me: could it have been the inspiration for this ghoulish atrocity? I often wonder who would want to live with it and where it is hanging now (owing to my notes being destroyed, the name of this weird artist escapes me).

Vanessa was supposed to be a good art critic. She had put Mervyn Peake on the map, but then he was, for all his grotesques, so amusingly clever. He would also do excellent straight painting, dismissed by Vanessa as photographic rubbish, a slap at commercial art – who was I to argue? Poor Vanessa was very scathing of my taste in art. One of the things I got the greatest enjoyment out of during those days was the Christmas window display in the Galeries Lafayette. All the windows were given over to automated, life-size kangaroos at a musical evening, dressed in the period of Napoleon Buonaparte. They even had joeys dressed as children of that period: the perfection of the setting fascinated me. The other was a large shop window with the most beautiful teddy-bears with brown fur, complete with chamois soles to their feet. They were arranged with a huge bear nearly as big as myself sitting in the centre, flanked on either side by graduated bears in V formation, coming down to either side of the shop window. It was clever window dressing, making my own and every other bear-fancier's mouth water: the prices were beyond all reason. For this humble bit of window-gazing I was well and truly castigated.

We progressed to see another genius from America, a pallid, Christ-like, bearded youth in toeless sandals, dirty slacks and cowboy shirt, who picked his nose incessantly. His exhibition was in a dirty, dusty little shop up a side street near St Jean de la Pauvre, that delightful little gem of a Greek Orthodox church with its famous acacia tree. At the shop entrance a long queue slowly inched its way round an upright block of wood standing dead centre of the completely empty, dark little shop. On this perched a very highly polished piece of hard wood like red mahogany. The base was approximately the size of an ostrich egg with the bottom sawn off it so it sat squarely on the block. Stuck in the middle of this egg was an excrescence the size of a hen egg. On top of the base was another oval the size of a goose egg, all carved out of one piece of wood. The critics and Press had their notebooks out, their agony and their ecstasy exuding positively from their pores at such beauty and magnificence. I looked and looked and my wonder grew at how the general public could be so stupid. As children we made much more excitingly realistic shapes out of the malformed potatoes known in Irish as polkerees.

'Now,' said Vanessa, 'you have seen real art today. In future don't go in for all this old master stuff.' At the ridiculous prices these horrors were fetching, it was highly unlikely that I would 'go in' for anything. Amongst the crowd of worshippers was a decent, normal-looking American. He caught my eye and winked. Having educated me in art, Vanessa left me to my own devices. I went to St Jean de la Pauvre, for sentimental reasons (Guy and I used to go there), thinking that when the crowd thinned out I could further investigate this potato-like carving, not daring to ask the oracle what it was meant to be. On my return visit the only people there were the sculptor and the American, the latter staring at it and fingering his chin thoughtfully. I asked him 'What in the name of all that's holy is that supposed to be?'

'Well, honey, I had to ask the same question, but not of my companion as he is a leading art critic so I came to see for myself. Would you believe it is a Madonna and Child?' We both laughed at our ignorance and fine fear of our separate mentors. Critics can make or mar a play, artist or writer, calling these abortions I had been shown top-class art.

Many years later my dear friend Freda Bruce Lockhart, the famous film and theatre critic, was staying with me the week the new Abbey Theatre in Dublin was opened. She expressed a wish to see a good Abbey play, so we sallied forth to see *Juno and the Paycock*, with all the Abbey top brass in the cast. It was a week after the Cork Film Festival so there were many continental critics in the audience. Freda slept solidly through the first act, which was magnificent. The applause woke her and in a very clear, carrying voice she announced 'Ham acting!' It echoed and rang through the auditorium. My aunt and I were sure we would be lynched. So much for critics.

My American friend took me out for dinner, much amused by my wanting to go down to Les Halles to find out about the south-going *camions* for next day. His French was excellent and he was most helpful and found that the best place to go was the Porte de Tailly by 7 am. Next morning I was on my way south in a vegetable lorry.

The first lift took me to Chartres, where I was able to explore the cathedral and its beautiful windows. It was rather spoilt for me as there had been a wedding the day before and the flowers were dying with that musty smell, plus the stench of the coffin of a notable who was reposing there before his state funeral later on in the day – not a good advertisement for the undertaker. The next lift took me to the tiny medieval town of Mer, where my driver assured me the nuns would give me a night's lodging. Did they, hell! They slammed the grille in my face, telling me that gipsies were not welcome. A passer-by told me to cross the Loire by the Château de Colliers bridge which was used as an *Auberge de Jeunesse*. The warden, a surly, grasping Frenchman, learning I had no money and was not a member of the Youth Hostellers Association, tried to throw me out. I told him I would work – that softened him.

All the other backpackers were foreign students. We cooked our own food in the kitchen and had to use an outside latrine in the vast courtyard. Our dormitory was in the attics, reached by a spiral staircase which was a dreadful fire hazard. The main part of the château was closed off. The beds were ten straw pallets on wooden frames with barely room to move between them. My traveller's cheques, passport and other small valuables I pushed down to the bottom of my fleabag. After about an hour, I felt a hand fumbling about under my pillow. It drew blank. In the dim moonlight from the dormer windows, I saw a shadowy figure moving from bed to bed. As he neared the door all hell was let loose. The rat population awoke for their moonlight steeplechase over the beds, which were only a few inches off the floor. It was like the Witches Frolic in the *Ingoldsby Legends* – 'Up jumped the cook, the potboy, the scullion', with just as much disarray. There must have been about fifty rats jumping about over the beds. In the *mêlée*, the shadowy figure merged with the crowd which ran screaming to the door; shining my torch on them, I distinctly saw the warden going out with the others. When all was quiet, I had a good night's sleep.

Realising that I would be framed if he had taken anything of value from the others, as I was now alone in the dormitory, I set my tiny alarm clock for 6 am. Quietly dressing, I crept down the stairs and was in the village by 7 am. Getting a lift to Tours, I broke my fast, lashing out on croissants and coffee well laced with cognac. I pottered around Tours and then made tracks for the open road. The next lift took me to St Maure, whence my Seymour ancestors originated in the Dark Ages. I had to walk a few kilometres for a lift to Poitiers: it was then getting dark, so I found a clean-looking café. The patron was an amiable fellow, his very pregnant wife was dead tired. I said I would help wash up all the clutter if they would give me a kip. They fed me and told me I could have the maid-of-all-work's bed, as she had been taken to the fever hospital that afternoon with polio. Politely declining, I said I would prefer to sleep in a chair in the kitchen. They were nice, kindly people. The wife went to bed, the man went to play cards with his pals, leaving me in sole possession of the café, now closed. In the morning they gave me coffee and croissants and put a small cheese and more croissants in a bag to support me during the day.

Some medical students bound for the Cameroons picked me up, taking me as far as Angoulême. After that I was out of luck. That cheerless country with the torrential rain was bothersome. Wandering into the pine woods, where there was comparative shelter, I found a farmhouse, heavily fortified. At last a nasty looking old chap with a deep sea cap poked his head out of the shutter in one of the very heavy doors and growled at me when I asked for shelter. He grudgingly sold me six bad potatoes and three onions. He filled my billycan half with milk, grabbed his twenty francs and slammed the shutter. I dined off potato and onion soup and strong tea and slept the sleep of the weary snug in a burrow of pine needles over my fleabag. It was fine and the air was crisp in the morning. More tea, the remains of Madame's croissants and I was on my way to

Bordeaux. Little did I know that the farmer was the man who with his son had murdered the poor Hamilton family, a *cause célèbre* of the time.

Two hops took me to Bordeaux. I stayed the night at a nice clean *Auberge de Jeunesse*: my fellow travellers were multi-lingual and told me they were on an archaeological trip and had found underground caves thirty kilometres west of Bordeaux, in which were prehistoric remains and spears and axeheads of the same epoch. They said they were the first humans to enter the caves since the inundation about three thousand years ago. It took them several hours crawling on their bellies to get into them and they hoped eventually to open them to the public. I have since read articles on these caves.

Next day I got a friendly driver to take me on the long haul to Dax. He told me he would fix me up with a pal of his who had a telephone repair van and was going to Biarritz and St Jean de Luz in the morning. The rain was absolutely pouring down and Dax, with its hot springs, was one of the creepiest towns I have ever been in: vapour from the springs rising to meet the rain seemed to take on the most dreadfully weird shapes. Standing outside the iron railings looking in, I could well imagine how these apparitions were conjured up in people's minds, especially if they were fasting as I was. The wet cobblestones made iridescent in the rain, scudding clouds leaving shafts of moonlight, the whole place was unearthly. I was glad to get into a small hotel for the night.

Next morning I picked up my friendly telephone man and off we chugged in the early morning, six of us stuffed into a cab which had a double seating arrangement. On the back of the huge *camion* were masses of telegraph poles. It was a very high vehicle which gave one a great view of the countryside. My five companions were all middle-aged men, all ex-soldiers and very kind. I laughed as we steamed into fashionable Biarritz to imagine what the Lady Mother would have said if she had seen the company her daughter was keeping.

It was now five o'clock and there was that clear, brittle, golden light of a November evening after rain. The harbour at St Jean de Luz was cobalt blue, the colourful little sailing craft swinging gently with the tide, the backdrop of the Pyrenees topped with snow like royal icing, the whole scene so peaceful with no tourists or rich playboys to shatter the idyll with their supercharged sportscars or overblown floozies. I would hate to go back there now and see it overrun with humanity. It was snowing now, in showers, the clouds chasing each other to reveal the deepest indigo blue sky dotted with myriads of dazzling stars. As I climbed the road to Hendaye, the air became so clear you felt you could put your hand out and stroke the velvet sky and pick a star to light your way.

At Hendaye the surly French customs man prodded and poked everything I had and then told me the border was closed until Monday. It was now nine o'clock on Saturday night and he should be off-duty. He expected a tip – blessed are those who expect nothing. That night and Sunday night I slept on the station platform, much to the distress of a kindly gendarme, spending most of Sunday in the station buffet, as it was warm, where I caught up with my writing. Every day when possible I wrote to my father in diary form, sending him the whole lot once a week. This reduced my luggage and would, I hoped ensure a faithful record of events.

At 7.45 am the border post was opened and I stepped on to Spanish soil, where so many of my fellow countrymen had voluntarily given their lives. A muleteer with a long cart drawn by two splendid mules gave me a lift into San Sebastian. It was the most uncomfortable part of the trip so far: the iron-shod wheels of the unsprung cart and the mules' trotting at a good clip of five to six miles an hour exacerbating the already bad roads. I rang my friend Lily to tell her I had nearly made it and she told me to take the train next day to Bilbao.

San Sebastian was a delightfully clean town, beautifully laid out, with a superb view down every street, the Atlantic sparkling down one vista, the mountains and countryside down the others. It was, in 1950, a small town unspoilt by tourism. The palms and other ornamental trees had been put into their winter wraps to protect them from the storms and frost. Feeling expansive, I wandered into a bodega for half a litre of red wine to wash down my tortilla. As I was enjoying my drink which cost me about six pesetas, (the pesata then being priced at four pence sterling), a frowsy female slung about with ancient camera and notebook pounced on me. She had never seen a backpacker, let alone a lone female of doubtful years: in Spain a woman over thirty was distinctly *passé*, and one who wandered about on her own was beyond all help. The lady journalist burbled at me in a delightful mixture of Spanish, French and incoherent English. Just for the hell of it, I pointed to the flash on my coat, speaking a few words of Irish. That threw her. She flew like a scalded cockerel, coming back a few minutes later with a novice priest. They both thought I was speaking in a Basque dialect, as many of the words in Irish are similar (the Basque fishermen and the County Waterford fishermen can converse). They got in a great state, looking at their watches, trying to tear me away from my wine, which I was thoroughly enjoying while I contemplated where I should spend the night. Now being virtually in a police state I had to mind my Ps and Qs. Eventually finishing my wine, I agreed to go to the newspaper office provided they gave me food and a night's lodging. The office was manned by novice priests and a very fat ordained one who sat, or rather overflowed, on a high stool, dabbing large sticky fingers into an archaic typewriter. This he continued to do as my escorts gabbled at him. To everything they said, he replied, 'No!' 'No photographs, señora, no article' – then when asked if he could get me lodging – 'No'. Then the lady said she knew the very place. We toiled up a steep hill on which sat the Convent of the Sisters of Charity. The Quire Sister in charge of vagrants was taken aback, suggesting I would be more comfortable in a hotel.

First I was shown into a long and spotless dormitory with twenty hospital-type beds with red and white blankets and coarse linen sheets, all spotless. The floor was highly polished red tiles, the walls snow white. It looked a Dutch interior from the brush of some old master. Supper was at 7 pm. I was then taken to the Prioress to sign the register. Looking at me quizzically, she called for 'Sister somebody'. An old crippled nun with the map of Ireland on her face hobbled into view. She hugged me, the tears running down her ivory cheeks – I was the first Irish person she had talked to since the Civil War. A native of County Limerick, she had been professed in Louvain after the First World War and was then sent to look after refugees at various convents in Belgium and France, ending up in charge of the vagrants in her present convent in 1933. She was multi-lingual but her English was halting as she did not get much chance to use it. It was mainly continental refugees who passed through. She was very amused at my adventures.

We all assembled in the dining-room for supper. The other inmates, about a dozen men and fourteen women plus a few literally stinking, louse-ridden children and babies, my companions, were drawn from all walks and conditions of life, including jailbirds, with their hair still cropped (both sexes) and prostitutes (several female, one or two gentlemen of the same persuasion). A beautiful, Madonna-like young nun in white from head to toe stood at the end of the refectory table to say the Rosary. In my childhood I had heard it recited both in our own and other people's kitchens at varying degrees of speed. This nun should have been in the *Guinness Book of Records* for a speed performance. Her voice purred like a flamenco-dancer's castanets, hardly pausing for response. We had grace at equal speed. Then it was like 'housey-housey', eyes down, look in and everyone, including myself, fell on their supper like wolves. It consisted of a large tin plate of soup and brown bread, the soup made of pea flour, sour milk, garlic and a little onion, piping hot and very good. This was followed by the same plate filled with an excellent brown bean stew, also piping hot and very satisfying, washed down by real spring water. Another grace, and then we were permitted to go to the spotlessly clean washroom and our dormitories at 8.30.

I was the only one allowed to take anything with me; all the others were literally frisked for everything but toothbrushes and combs. There were only two others in my dormitory: a prostitute and a Polish refugee. Both thought I was too silly to have a strip wash in cold water, and to change into pyjamas was the end of all snobbery!

After another cool wash at 7.30 am, I stripped my bed, packed up my belongings and was read for the off. Breakfast consisted of a big hunk of brown bread with a huge bowl of hot dried milk flavoured with vanilla. It sounds awful, but was really good. After the Rosary and grace, again at a rate of knots, a white nun made signs that I was to follow her. The Limerick nun wanted to see me. She had lost a brother in the 1916 Dublin Rebellion and another at Guernica in the Spanish Civil War. She presented me with a faded envelope in which was an oak leaf from the famous tree in Guernica where the two wolves appear when there is going to be a disaster. The leaf, which had been sent to her by her brother, had the wolves worked into it. (There is a special name for such work on dried leaves, which escapes me.) Later I got some Spanish friends to photograph the tree and the well to send to her. A year later they told me she had died shortly after receiving it.

Feeling like a giant refreshed with wine, I decided to walk along the coast road for about two kilometres, and a further nine down a lovely valley to Usubil, where I caught the train to Bilbao.

On the road my rucksack had caused great interest amongst the shoals of bicycle-riding factory workers holding up their umbrellas to keep off the morning mist. They looked like a lot of mobile black mushrooms. The train, with its other passengers, could well have been the Skibbereen to Clonakilty line or the Lartigue railway between Ballybunion and Listowel, carrying the shawled ladies with their baskets of produce, cans of milk or unfortunate live hens hung by their legs or baskets of quacking ducks, with even a small piglet adding his voice to the cacophony. The same gossip, banter and leg-pulling, was exchanged, and faces could well have been those of handsome Kerry women.

Lilian Fallon and Nancy Cameron met me at the station, very relieved girls at seeing me all in one piece. Bilbao was a small town once famous for its steelworks, but now it seemed to exist rather than thrive. The milk-vendors from the surrounding country came in each morning with their strings of donkeys like disjointed rosaries: only one animal per string had a rope head-collar, their milk-cans slung on either side of them. Cans empty, they headed for home, the lady owner sitting sideways on the hindquarters of the last donkey, usually the one with the headrope on.

The shops were full of the Christmas displays, cheap and tawdry. The chief Christmas sweetmeat was a light-coloured marzipan snake coiled up. These varied in price from a couple of pesetas to the equivalent in sterling of several pounds. The snake in the south of Spain is taboo not only as unlucky but representing sin. I found the Basques hard, tough, insular people, completely different from the Andalusians and southern Spanish, as the north of Ireland people are from us southerners, the feud then nearly as bitter as it is now but kept well under control by the Franco regime. The rich were very rich, the poor very poor. What would be the equivalent of middle-class professional people's standard and lifestyle was only that of small shopkeepers in an English village. The rich people's babies were muffled up to the eyebrows, with their little made-up olive-skinned faces giving them a peculiar appearance, to be carried to the squares by their nannies for an airing. All nannies wore long earrings of coloured balls. Some had only one earring, others two, the difference, which I cannot now remember, denoting a wet-nurse.

We went to a watch-night service in the main church on Christmas Eve. The colour, the incense, the candles, vestments, priests and choir as they processed, the jewels glittering in the candlelight, all gave it an unearthly appearance, for except for the altar and processional candles the whole church was in darkness. At the stroke of midnight the lights flashed on, the Star of Bethlehem shone over the High Altar and underneath it a trap-door flew open to reveal the Holy Baby, his arms outstretched – all superbly stage-managed. The way he shot out reminded me, irreverently, of a cuckoo-clock. Next to where I sat was the glass coffin of a saint, or at least the poor chap's bones. He too was lit up.

On Christmas Day we ate inkfish and a middle-sized marzipan snake for our Christmas dinner. On Boxing Day we went to tea with Spanish friends, the Ajurias: we were again given Spanish cooking at its richest, with delightful cakes and tortilla. The Ajuria girls' father was chairman and part owner of Novaera Aznar, a coastal shipping company. The fleet varied from large, ocean-going vessels to the dirty little tramps 'with the salt-caked smokestacks' of about 500 tons, plying their trade round the coasts of Spain and Portugal. When they heard my plan to hitch-hike across Spain, they were horrified, because even then there were real brigands in the mountains. Señor Ajuria offered me an alternative, which was to sail on the *Montebustello*: the captain was an old friend of his who spoke perfect English, or as perfect as one could with a strong Cardiff accent. His ship was in Barry docks for the whole of the Spanish Civil War, not being allowed to return home, and she earned her keep by plying her trade up and down the west coast of England with the occasional trip across the Irish Sea. The *Montebustello* was 500 tons and was indeed the epitome of the dirty little tramp, calling at fifteen ports en route for Barcelona. I would eat the ship's food, have a clean bunk, and see all the ports she called at for £35, the trip lasting four weeks. This would leave me with some money in hand owing to what I had eased out of Ireland.

Nancy came up the night before I sailed from Santander and we were able to see the wonderful cave drawings outside the town which had not been discovered so very long. Between Santander and Musel, the next port of call, the Bay of Biscay began to get a bit saucy. The crew and the captain were not interested in food and in their own words 'changed the peseta' pretty often over the side. The ship was a gallant little vessel, riding the ridge and furrow like a good 'un but shipping it pretty green, when the waves came over the bows, at the same time.

All eyes were on the strange woman. The officers consisted of Johnny Sparks, the radio operator, Paulina A'que, the first mate and bosun, and Vincente, the engineer, who did not eat with us. He was an old school friend of the captain's and very good to me although he spoke no English. The poor chaps, I felt sorry for their green faces. As usual in a rough at sea, I suffered from an insatiable appetite. The food was varied, as the captain jokingly said. No breakfast except for me: toasted bread as hard as a rock and villainous black coffee made of God knows what. By lunchtime I was roaring like a lion with hunger. For lunch we had beans and fish; for supper, by way of variety, we had fish and beans. This was really a type of paella with everything mixed into it on one huge plate. The menu got a bit more variety when we entered the Med., as the steward could get those poor little sparrow-like birds cooked to death in the galley on skewers. The bosun would eat his like asparagus, inserting the skewers full length into his open mouth, pulling out the skewer and crunching up the entire bird – beak, bones, legs, the lot, like the old man in Alice. We also got a rather tasteless red fish on the bone which he subjected to the same treatment.

Our first port was Musel, the port for Gijon, which was about six kilometres away by train. There I saw a pauper's funeral – plain wooden box and rickety hearse – the horse and driver both so frail and old they might have been two of Hogarth's dogs. The plume on the poll-strap of the horse was so worn it looked a superannuated bottlebrush. The priest's vestments were filthy; these he dragged from two equally dirty little altar-boys who ran across a field to the waiting hearse. Walking in front of the hearse, they then unfurled the flags they were carrying and the *cortège* was on its decrepit way up the hill.

I also visited the bacalao factory: bacalao is one of the staple dishes, being dried, salted cod mostly caught in Irish waters. It is salted and dried in ovens or kilns on racks like clothes in a dress shop. These racks are wheeled out to the cooling-off room and the fish is then packed for distribution. It is the same thing as ling, which is found in every Irish kitchen, a chunk being cut off it on Thursday to soak in time for Friday's dinner. I must say it was not quite so salty and stringy in Spain. This factory was looked upon as a showpiece. The workers were given two kilos of bacalao twice weekly and a good meal in the canteen with half a litre of wine every day for the equivalent of tuppence three-farthings (about 1p).

Passing El Ferrol, which looked like Crosshaven harbour with Carrigaline and Carrigtohill on either side, in due course we came into Vigo where we had to stand off outside in a heavy fog as it was tricky getting into the lagoon-like harbour. Once in, you could conceal the whole British fleet, and owing to the treacherous entrance there is untold wealth sunk in its very deep waters.

After two days' steady steaming down the length of the Portuguese coast, we came to the mouth of Guadalquivir River, up which we were to sail to Seville. The captain was worried which pilot he would get as one was often drunk and the other blind. The latter had landed them on a sandbank on a previous trip and the former ran down a cow that was being swum across the river at low tide. Fortunately we got a good pilot who spoke English and allowed me on the bridge with him. Between him and the captain it was a wonderfully informative trip, up the longest navigable river in Europe. In some places the river was so narrow that the ship's company could converse with the local residents. At sundown it was indescribably beautiful. First came the flat salt-marshes on the port side, with small thatched hovels in compounds on the starboard side. This gave way to the paddy-fields, with their sparkling mounds of salt, and rich pastures containing herds of the most carefully bred fighting bulls on the other side. Finally, there were small hamlets and orange groves, and as the light faded to the west, and the heat of the day subsided, the delicious smell of orange blossom wafted across the river. The moon and stars high in the sky contrasted vividly with the translucent light in the west. Combined with the Moorish style of architecture, the Arabic music coming over the ship's wireless and the cows being swum across the river to their homesteads for the night, the whole would have made a perfect setting for an eastern musical comedy.

Seville was a beautiful old town steeped in Moorish and religious history. Vincente, the ship's engineer, was related to the then ruling church dignitary of the Cardinal, Seguria, known half in jest and half in earnest as Pedro the Cruel, who had been a strict and not too gentle ruler of Seville. The Cardinal was a Spanish prototype of Father O'Flynn but he did not suffer fools gladly and allowed nothing to interfere with his *modus operandi*. Coming of wealthy people, he spent much of his own fortune helping the poor. He also disapproved of the enormous wealth which the Church had stored in their treasure-houses when there was so much desperate need.

Out of his own pocket he had built what was jokingly known as 'his hotel', a large and uncompromising block of apartments on some waste land outside the town. These had all mod. cons. and were allotted to the destitute with young families or to the old and infirm. Those able, were found employment and if they did not work they soon found themselves back where they started. He personally inspected the place every so often.

Having visited all the famous sights of the town, Paulina and I went to the poor gipsy quarter across the river to the church of the Virgin, Dolores La Triana, where we were shown the bull-fighters' beautiful suits of lights as well as all the gold and jewels in the church treasury. The sacristan was a beautiful gipsy girl who kept looking at me in a peculiar way and then asked Paulina if I was 'one of them'. He was rather shocked, when I told her through him that way back in my family there was gipsy blood on both sides, but she was over the moon, embracing me fondly and refusing to take the customary tip or allowing us to put anything in the offertory box.

On the last evening we went to a *bodega*, a very rough sailors' dive where knifing and prostitution abounded. There the huge sherry vats were buried in clay and had beehive hats for extra coolness. Sherry, ice-cold and clear as crystal, was served to the most seasoned drinkers in tiny, tall glasses no bigger than a liqueur glass. The company was bizarre to say the least of it, and scenes like this made me regret not being an artist so I could set them down for posterity. The remarks and questions about me as a great curiosity were, I believe, too personal for the captain or Paulina to repeat verbatim, but by then I had got a fair idea of the language, although I was still unable to speak it. I was able to work my way in the daily papers with the aid of a dictionary.

In the morning, before we left, the captain raced me up to Hiralgo. No one is allowed to go up on their own owing to the many suicides. Two Americans fighting over money did not stop the battle of the dollar to let us get past, and we were then followed by a very agitated guide who thought now that the knives were out and that they had caused our headlong flight to the top. We saw the court of dolls, the Sultan's harem, where the ten wives had their separate windows looking out on to the court. I found it creepily heavy with sensuality, cruelty and depression in spite of the beautiful proportions of the building.

Leaving Seville, we headed back along the coast south to Cadiz.

With the old women sitting outside their doors, small children clamped between their knees as they explored their heads for livestock, the outskirts could well have been any small fishing village on the west coast of Ireland. Here we took on board a pompous, rich gent. of doubtful origin, ablaze with diamonds and armed with his own personal and private eunuch.

We also picked up a major on his way back to barracks in Tetuán via Ceuta, our next port, on the north Moroccan coast. Ceuta was a dreary little village full of cheap brothels. The major asked the captain and me to go to Tetuán and dine in the Mess. It would have been very interesting but there was a riot on when we arrived – in a rather antiquated staff-car – so as well as dining we had to stay the night in barracks, never seeing any of the town, but making a dash back for Ceuta early in the morning. The ship's company was sure we had been abducted and that, even though Morocco was still a Spanish mandate, they would have an international situation on their hands.

It was snowing heavily when we got back, and in the afternoon they took me on a round of the brothels. The poshest one was owned by an Anglo-Indian madam who spoke English. She proudly showed me her business premises and her girls, mostly of Middle East origin. Also, quite unabashed, she showed me all the tools of her trade, catering for every taste, creed, colour or perversion, including the older girls whose front teeth had been extracted for oral sex. She gave us some delicious Arab sweetmeats and mint tea, showing me how to make it and how to hold the scalding glass without burning my hands. It dawned on me why mint was so favoured, because in stud work peppermint mint used to be fed to stallions to increase their fertility. Looking up my herb book afterwards, I found that in the Middle Ages mint was used not only for fertility but as an aphrodisiac. The girls, who were regularly medically inspected, seemed happy enough as it was better than living in doorways and their futures were ensured in a convent when they passed their prime. Madam, who was well into her sixties, was reputed to be the daughter of a famous English general who had served in India. The captain told me there was some truth in this, since he had taken high-ranking English people to Ceuta who were related to her and had helped to set her up in business. Certainly nothing changes down the ages.

Our next port of call on the southern Spanish coast, Málaga the Beautiful, really lived up to its name. As I sipped my *vino tostada* at a café overlooking the bay, a good-looking, very well-tailored man of about thirty-five came in and came straight over to me and introduced himself as a doctor, speaking English with a heavy German accent. He was a pure gipsy and had qualified in Germany during the Spanish Civil War. He took me to the *gitanas'* old settlement in Málaga, which he looked after. They had their own church and their own laws, but I was made as welcome as one of themselves. They were very clean, the rich ones helping their poorer brethren. He took me into a tent where he had delivered a baby early that morning. It lay in its mother's arms like a bright-eyed little marmoset monkey. The midwife, an old lady with a wonderful face, was sitting at the door of the tent. She had worked in a maternity hospital during the Civil War, coming back to her own people afterwards. The doctor said she was as good at her job as any highly trained hospital nurse. She curtsied deeply to me, never taking her eyes off my face, and said: 'Señora has seen great happiness, also great sorrow. There is much unhappiness in store for you but you will overcome it. Then there will be peace in a place of beauty and many, many trees. You will never be rich but will know the happiness of true friendship, and the love of your animals.'

We were away so long that the captain was getting *agitato*, but the doctor reassured him on our return. I asked the doctor how he knew me and he said: 'We have our own telegraphic system. The sacristan in La Triana passed the word.'

The telegraph system obviously worked as far as Almeria, our next stop, for here three full-blooded, well-dressed gipsies met me on the quay when the ship docked and took me up the mountains – bare of all vegetation – to the wonderful caves of their relatives. The caves looked nothing from the outside but inside they were according to the wealth and status of their owners like well-appointed salons: electric light, Persian rugs, divans, and in the bigger, more opulent ones, fountains playing from sculpted nymphs or fishes in marble basins in the centre. Openings off the main rooms were sleeping and cooking areas. One of the largest was owned by an elderly lady who in her youth had been a very famous flamenco dancer and was, they told me, a millionairess. After some refreshment and wine, she gave me an impromptu performance. Old by their standards she may have been, but her movements had lost nothing of their fluidity and sinuous grace. Her castanets positively purred. Dressed in full gipsy dancing regalia, she looked stunning.

I was escorted back to the ship, where the gipsies told the captain that they wanted me to come that night to a very special gipsy ceremony. They would fetch me and bring me back but it would be very late. Poor chap, he got in a dither when they left. He could not believe I was not afraid to go alone with them. I reassured him about my safety, and in due course set off with my escort up a different part of the mountain. This turned out to be to the funeral party of a child, the son of extremely wealthy people. The cave was lit up like a Walt Disney set, with a beautiful fountain playing in the salon and a feast laid out on priceless carved tables, set at either side of what I at first took to be an effigy or large doll sitting in its little chair. It was the child for whom the farewell party was organised. Dressed in splendour wth his face made up, like an American mortician's beauty treatment, it gave me the creeps. At the same time, although the thought was macabre, there was no melancholia about the proceedings. The boys played and sang lovely, haunting gipsy airs and music and the castanets purred as the dancers whirled. When my escorts explained to me what it all meant had it not been for the *corpus delecti* it would have been a delightful evening.

At the height of the gaiety the whole company froze, looking out into the night. Seated a few yards from the entrance was a large fox, his eyes fixed on me, as were all the human eyes. Raising his mask, he gave the three staccato barks in a tone I knew so well, when tragedy is going to overtake my family. Having given his warning, he turned and walked away until he merged into the shadow of the lava slopes. The whole company surrounded me, saying, 'You are of the foxes.' The fox had not been seen in that area for many years. I felt shaken, and worried that something might be going to happen to my father, who was not in the best of health, but the gipsies reassured me it was no one close to me.

On arrival at Barcelona, my next mail pick-up, there was a letter from my father to say that my beloved Siamese cat was found dead in a snare on the night the fox came to warn me.

After brief stops at Cartagena and Alicante, we came to Valencia, a very Moorish city where the people speak their own Sicilian language.

It was here that I went to a bullfight. I do feel that, whatever, else he may have done, Franco did a lot of necessary cleaning up, not least of which was to insist that the bullfighting horses were properly padded and protected and that they wore blinds and did not have their eyes put out, as was so commonly stated. Before the fight, I was taken behind the scenes into both the human and animal surgeries, whose operating theatres were immaculate with a qualified doctor and veterinary surgeon in attendance. The people who howl and rage about fox-hunting do so without any real knowledge of how a carnivorous predator exists in the wild. The same people rant and rave about the cruelty of bullfighting, without knowledge. The bulls who are selected get every care, and woe betide the handlers if the bull goes into the ring with a mark or a blemish on it from a stick. The fight can last anything from ten to twenty minutes and then it is all over. Should the *coup de grâce* not be perfect, the bull is immediately shot. To compare his life and that of our cattle is ludicrous. The people who make such a fuss about bullfighting should see the French, Belgian and Eastern bloc abattoirs for horses and cattle, which are too horrible for words. Our own poor cattle are beaten into lorries and if one goes down it is just too bad, and it is the farmer's loss if it gets trampled to death. Driven at speed, they are then whacked out of the lorry, slipping and sliding in filth and blood, and belted across the nose to stop them escaping out of the yard or crush. They are starved for twenty-four hours so are hungry and thirsty as well as frightened. Who are we to criticise a situation where a well-cared-for, well-fed animal displays his courage and meets a clean death having been fed and watered that very morning? But even though they are padded, I still do not like the horses being used.

To see a top-class toreador working is like watching a Russian ballet; every pass of the cape means something. Here in Valencia the bull-ring is very fine but as it was not the fashionable season we only saw three *novicios* and an old hand who was trying to come back. Before I left Spain I heard he had been killed, badly gored several times. He had lost his nerve and it showed in the way he went about the job – and the bulls obviously knew it.

After a brief trip across to the beautiful and luscious island of Mallorca, we arrived at our final destination, Barcelona, the second city of Spain. The first thing you see is that arch mischief-maker Christopher Columbus on his pillar pointing to the New World.

The Spaniards did not like him, spreading the rumour that he was born in a brothel. I had made great plans to explore all the museums and art galleries after I left the ship, but Matthew put paid to this. Among my package of mail was a cryptic *communiqué* from him telling me in his own words: 'Seeing you sooner than expected in circumstances other than I could wish. Go home at once; find a job and somewhere to live.' The captain let me sleep aboard for two nights but I had only a superficial look at this very lovely city, which was then still suffering from the Civil War like a badly mauled king of the jungle licking his wounds.

On the last night I took the captain to hear *Parsifal* sung by a good Italian company. Although I had seen more of Spain and the real way of life then, I had not touched on the very rich or the grandees. The opera-house, which is reckoned second to La Scala, lived up to its reputation. It was huge and magnificent with excellent acoustics. The grandees and their señoras in stalls and dress circles were magnificent in their jewelled opulence.

As the captain and all the crew had bent over backwards to help me, I thought I would give them a treat before packing my traps, so I went to a big delicatessen at the top of the Plaza de las Ramblas. Whilst struggling with my Spanish, a little bald-headed man popped out of his office, rushed round the counter, grabbed my hand and, beaming at me, asked: 'And when were you in Cork last?' His father had trained his three sons in the business and had sent them to Jacksons in Piccadilly, Findlaters in Dublin and this one to Smith Stores in Cork. He took us into his office giving us wine and sweetmeats, and would not hear of taking a penny for what I wanted, which he had packed and sent down to the ship. The captain told him I was an extraordinary woman to be travelling alone, the more so as I was not sick in the Bay. 'Ah, my friend,' the grocer said, 'she would never be seasick – was she not brought up on the Douglas trams?' Later I had to explain that the said trams were notorious the world over for their rocking and swaying motion and were the butt of every music-hall joke.

I owe a very big thank-you to Señor Ajuria, Captain Jesus Eelav and first mate Paulina A'que. But for them I would not have seen Spain as it was and never will be again, now that it has become a fashionable resort. All the Spaniards were very curious then, asking me lots of intimate questions, but the one that always turned up was: 'Have you seen the King and Queen of England and do they walk about?' There was an intense longing amongst all classes to have their monarchy restored.

With great sadness I left Barcelona by the night train, returning to a wet and still war-weary London. I got a job within twenty-four hours as a housekeeper in a girls' club, the Helena Club, where I stayed for the next three months. Matthew came back six weeks later, having been called on to resign his commission – he should have been cashiered. But from the day that he returned until I had great pleasure in divorcing him some years later, he never once asked about my trip or how I had fared in his absence. It is amazing in this day and age to think that I could have had that wonderful trip for just under £75.

# 16

# THE LAST ROUND-UP

As Matthew was kicked out of the Army after his disgraceful conduct in Hong Kong and Korea (he had been in association with the notorious Hong Kong police force, then known to be the most corrupt in the Colonies; and in Korea he had refused to obey an order in the face of the enemy, thereby putting his men in danger), I was then the breadwinner for the family. The late Arthur Wilkinson, a stud farmer and old friend from before the war, lent us one of his cottages at Didmarton in Gloucestershire and gave Erna grazing in return for me riding his stallions and keeping an eye on things for him while he was in hospital.

Erna was in very good condition when I had fetched her early in 1952 off the train at Badminton station, but her poor feet were in an awful state. Father, I suppose, had not felt up to it, and the Lady Mother had forbidden him to take the blacksmith to her regularly during the last year. It was my uncle who shipped her over to me, although Father was still well enough to hunt and attend to his farming.

We lasted at Didmarton about a year, then Matthew upset Arthur, not a difficult thing to do at the best of times, but the poor man was heading for the final breakdown in which he ended his life. We had only a fortnight to get out. Fortunately the mother of Pat Hewlett, an old veterinary friend of mine, had just bought the Old Rectory at Arlingham down on the Severn and was looking for someone to share it with her. Pat got us in there. Erna had a big paddock and stable all to herself. Her feet were getting better with regular shoeing, although Major Duncan, my old vet, advised rest, suggesting I got her in foal. Nothing we could do seemed to work but gradually she became sound and rideable again.

Our benefactress knew a lot of people in Stroud, so tales of

Matthew's extra-mural activities with the ladies of the town came back to her. Again we were asked to leave. This time there was nothing for it but to buy a caravan, which of course came out of my meagre savings.

We got a site from a farmer at Eastington, not far from Gloucester, down a very dirty lane, and another farmer took Erna in. All this time I was working at making loose covers and curtains. Whilst doing this for a terrific character in Stonehouse, one Joan Hayward of Haywards End (known to all the village as 'Miss Baby'), she offered me the four-acre field in front of her house for a caravan and Erna. She had been an ardent hunting woman in her day. The rent for the whole lot was £10 per annum on the strict understanding that the lease was in my name and *only* I knew what the rent was. Matthew never knew, nor did he care.

The second year we were there I had to have major surgery in Cheltenham General Hospital. During the two weeks I was there, Matthew sold Erna to the local knacker for £40. For once, his blowing and boasting did me a good turn. He shot his mouth off about his cleverness to Miss Baby who, bless her heart, told the knacker's man the mare was not Matthew's to sell. She had another friend take her away while Matthew was at work and they kept her until I came out of hospital. It must have been a scream because the knacker had paid Matthew, who had blown the money the night he got it. The old chap threatened to go to his boss or the police if it was not returned. Who Matthew touched for it I know not, but my guess is that they never got it back.

When I came out of hospital those kindly people the Berkeleys offered me the secretaryship of the Berkeley Hunt point-to-point: this entitled me to one day's hunting a week and a tiny honorarium plus expenses. Matthew, who had collected the sack again from the hydraulics factory where he was working, was in some kind of quasi-political job in London, gracing us with his presence most weekends. We were greatly relieved when his German-Jewish lady love claimed him full time.

After Matthew finally decamped, my old friends caught up with me again. Owing to his misconduct I had fought shy of contacting them, for I never knew what he would get up to next. Erna and I had many a happy day's hunting spent with them and their packs, as widely scattered as the Devon and Somerset Stag Hounds to Pickering in Yorkshire. She jumped everything with the ease and grace of a gazelle. It saddens me very much to think that 90 per cent of those kindly people have, like my beloved mare, all gone to join the great majority.

We had a very good hunt one Saturday from Whitminster, Erna going like the proverbial bomb. I was always very careful of her in rough or stony ground as one sole was thin. We had to cross a causeway over a rine (the very deep ditches that intersect the Berkeley country) which was laid down in hardcore made up of builder's rubble and broken bricks. I pulled her up to a walk to cross it when a well-known thruster hit her on her quarters, shouting at me for God's sake to get on and let him through. She plunged forward, landing on a broken brick and pitching on to her nose. We did not part company, but she just stood still with her off-fore held up in the air. It took me two hours to get her the three miles home. Major Duncan came out to her and diagnosed irreparable damage to the pedal bone. I was never able to hunt her again, although with special shoeing and a leather sole she was able to enjoy life without pain or lameness.

At the age of 12, Erna was still a comparatively young mare, so I determined to leave no stone unturned to get her in foal. When the late Maxie Cosgrove MRCVS (who was a childhood friend of mine) was in England, he came to examine her. He was not over-optimistic, but said that the old people's remedy would be the only hope – i.e. let a two-year-old colt run with her, for if he caught her right and she went in foal it would sort out her ovarian trouble, and hopefully we could send her to a thoroughbred the following year. After a pretty good search we found a two-year-old cart colt to run out with her.

One side of Erna's field in Stonehouse ran alongside the Bristol-Stroud road, the other being bordered by the fork off the main road to Stonehouse village. Everything that took place in her field was open to the public gaze. My friends and I were very amused when all the ladies complained about the shockingness of what went on. But whereas only about half a dozen normally went for their constitutionals along that road (known locally as the Monkey's 'Prade') on weekdays, its popularity suddenly became immense – hordes of the elderly and pram-pushers crowded the footpath, even waiting and watching for something to happen! Some complained about the indecency of the 'goings on' but it did not stop them walking that way. When the colt went home at the end of September, the Monkey's 'Prade' was nigh deserted.

While we lived in Stonehouse, Erna had her 'followers'. These she categorised into three groups: those who wanted to gape at her; the useful ones who produced bread, cake, apples or any fruit; and the ones who, when you were bored, you allowed to stroke your nose over the post-and-rail. Hoffmans Factory spewed out its day workers in a shower of cyclists at about 5.45 pm. Many of them had not eaten all their packed lunches. These they would offer to her over the hedge, calling: 'Horse, Horse, come here, Horse.' The sandwiches with pickles were not a favourite, so these she kindly left for the dogs and the birds, but she did go in a big way for cheese and onion, tomato or egg sandwiches (my three bull terriers got short-changed when these were on the menu). It was amusing to see her and the bull terriers converging at the bottom of the field at about 5.30 pm. She knew with unerring judgement who were time-wasters and who was good for a 'touch'.

The Planning Authorities started to get awkward about sites. By now I had built up quite a nice little antique business while working full-time as an appeals secretary, covering fifteen counties with an average day's driving of 300 miles. I had commissions to buy for several dealers, who came at the weekends to collect their goods. After ten years there, I tired of Stonehouse, which was rapidly becoming a very built-up area, so we made tracks for Wales, where the antique trade was booming with the growing tourist industry and the holiday homes people. We managed to get a cottage at Tregwent on the coast, with a safe garden for the dogs, and across the road space for my lovely Bluebird Safari caravan, a barn for the antiques, a box for Erna and two small paddocks of approximately six acres in all: the rent was £50 p.a.

I got several good lets for the caravan and was doing well with the antiques, selling on my own as well as keeping my trade contacts, and still getting orders for loose covers and curtains. Erna did not care for the place much as one of her little paddocks was very secluded from human contact, so except for the dogs and me she was a bit isolated.

There was a blacksmith about a mile away, whose forge overlooked the famous Blue Pool beyond the village of St Nicholas. The cliffs of the pool or bay were extremely sheer: to get to it in a boat you would have had to go from Aber Castle Bay. By now Erna was sound enough for me to ride her at a walk to the blacksmith. A lot of sheep were grazed on the heathery headlands. Back towards Tregwent a farmhouse had been sold to holiday people, the farmer retaining the surrounding land. They kept a few old screw horses to ride when they came down from Cardiff at weekends. The fields in that part of Wales were fenced with banks, similar to Irish banks, the boundary ones being high, stonefaced and narrow. For some time there had been mysterious sheep worrying, with sheep driven over the sheer cliff and some poor ewes heavy in lamb appearing to have been trampled or battered to death, but with no bites or tearing visible.

Since Erna had a sheep phobia, she normally kept well clear of them. However, on our way to the blacksmith one morning I saw one of the holiday people's screws jump the big boundary fence into the headland. Initially marvelling that he could jump so well, the next thing I saw was him making a beeline for the flock of sheep. I have never seen such savagery in a horse: he sent two fat lambs spinning over the cliff, then literally like a sheepdog cut two ewes from the now terrified flock. Erna was by now in hysterics, hearing the sheep bleating and seeing them rushing all over the headland. The old brute was now pounding one of the sheep into the ground. I yelled like a redskin at him but he took no notice. It was quite near 'Williams the Road''s cottage: yelling for someone to come quickly, his aged deaf wife came out just in time to see what was going on, but age and infirmity prevented her from doing anything to help. Having had his morning's fun, the old brute turned round and popped back over the fence. Leaving Erna in the forge, I went into the Post Office and phoned the police, sure in my mind that I had a witness. They came, found one carcass and the other badly injured ewe. When they asked 'William the Road''s wife about it she denied having *either* seen me or the event I described. One of the CID men who was a farmer's son asked me if I would show him where the horse had jumped the fence. My honour was vindicated, as apparently it was his usual spot for getting over into the sheep. They set a watch for him after that, and two days later caught him at it again. The CID man told me that Mrs Williams the Road would never admit to seeing the horse killing the sheep because her daughter was the owner's home help when they came down at weekends.

On the following Sunday I heard a cavalry charge coming up the road by my cottage. It was led by paterfamilias wearing chaps, a loud check shirt, sombrero hat hanging down his back and espadrilles on his feet. He was riding the miscreant, who was the weirdest looking horse I ever saw. He must have been about 15.2 hh, but nothing seemed to be in the right place. He had pony's ears stuck in the centre of his poll so that they flopped outwards, not forwards; his head was truly a coffin shape but big enough for an 18 hh Shire horse; and his piggy little eyes were right up in the top of his skull. Poor horse, he would have been right into Mervyn Peake's basket for grotesques.

The ladies (four of them), all buxom in the extreme, no holds barred, so to speak, were similarly attired as Daddy. Their Welsh ponies, on which they overflowed, were small. Erna, who was not only madly in use but also in her roadside paddock, came to stare at this wondrous sight. The killer, one Merlin by name, got one whiff of her, screeched, and proceeded to claw his way up the roadside wall of her field. Daddy slid backwards, hitting the deck pretty hard with his well-upholstered behind. They had come to attack me for laying evidence against Merlin. I shouted at them to take that damned rig away before he did any other damage. They did not understand what I meant. I tried to explain to them what was wrong with the poor horse, suggesting that he should either be sold to the knackers or see a vet, but that at his age it would be a risky operation. Mother twittered: 'But Mr Ryce Morgan sold him to us as a four-year-old because he was too good for his riding school!' I bet he was! He would never see fourteen, let alone four again.

Then Mother brazenly asked if they could borrow Erna for a friend the next weekend. Thinking me an old curmudgeon for refusing, they clattered off on their way, blissfully happy in their ignorance.

Once again on the way to the blacksmith, Erna was to witness another sheep happening. The foxes round Tregwent and Goodwich were literally in droves. Up the hill in front of my cottage was a nice flock of good, strong, fat lambs. In the field below them two men were loading bales of hay. I heard a row and, looking over the fence, saw four foxes attack and pull down a big ram lamb. The men heard nothing with the noise of the tractor engine. Eventually, when I got their attention, it took the two of them all they could do to beat the foxes off the lamb with their hayforks. They told me this foxpack hunting was nothing new round there. Much as Erna loved fox-hunting, she did not 'go' very much for the sheep side of things.

At the end of July 1965 the poor Lady Mother went to sleep in her chair after her afternoon tea, never to wake again. She never told anyone where I was, although I had given her my full address and also that of my bankers and solicitors. She was buried over a week when they finally traced me. This meant I could return to my native land with impunity, so in September Erna and I once again crossed the Irish Sea together.

The Lady Mother had sold our old home and disposed of everything, leaving nothing when she died but a very tatty bungalow. This I managed to sell and the following Spring bought my first little stud farm in County Tipperary. It is a county I never liked, but land, house and price were right. At the age of 23, Erna was still full of life, making her presence and seniority felt with the three foundation mares whom I had acquired. She led the herd: if one dared go through a gate ahead of her, they got a good nip for their pains and stood back respectfully. She had one spot on the farm that she made completely her own, a high mound near the house. From this she could command a view of the whole small outfit, missing nothing. Never very keen on the society of other horses, she strangely made a terrific friend of Scali Rua, a very beautiful chestnut mare. They were inseparable.

In early 1969 I noticed that Erna was not keeping her condition and was rather slow in getting up. One thing I have always held is that old horses feel the cold very much and that it is cruel to just pension them off, leaving them out all the year round with only a field shelter for protection against the weather. Like ageing people, they need warmth and the stimulus of companionship. Erna lacked none of these things, but she was well into her twenty-eight year. One morning in September she was lying down near her friend when I went to look at her. Pulling her ears and talking to her, I knew she must not be asked to go through another winter, even though she would be well fed and in a warm loose box. A few days later, as she was coming up to the yard leading the other mares, I thought I saw her stagger. It could have been over-anxiety on my part, or rough ground, but a week later I saw it again, no mistake this time. Then she could not get up in her box a few mornings later without a great struggle.

I called the vet, who gave her a thorough check-up, saying her heart was sound as a bell and it was only a touch of rheumatism; no need to worry. A very old friend of Erna's and mine came to stay on 24 November. The following morning we had a job to help Erna to get up. She who loved her food only picked at it in a half-hearted way, leaving it to look out of her box door. She turned around, staggered, and nearly fell over. That afternoon I went for the grave-diggers. The following morning the vet came. He gave her a sedative and when she was drowsy I led her out to her favourite spot where her grave now was. Then he gave her an intravenous injection which she did not feel. She just lay down quite naturally; then, again intravenously, the vet gave her a pint of Epsom salts and water. Poor old darling, she just slept herself away. Jan Norton, my friend, put her shield with all her army badges in her grave with her and then blew the Last Post and Reveille on my father's hunting horn.

So my beloved friend and companion of twenty-six years and I were parted for ever on 26 November 1969. We had had our ups and downs together, but even if I went without a few extras myself when times were bad, she never went short. She, I firmly believe, kept me sane through the ten years of my ghastly second marriage.

After her grave was filled in and properly sodded, the other mares were let into the field. It was an extraordinary sight: they who dared not encroach on her special lookout post crowded round the grave with heads bent as if in homage. When in that field, until we left the farm three years later, morning and evening they stood for a few minutes round the grave. Many people have seen this, remarking on it. For nearly a month her special friend Scali Rua stayed as close to the grave as she could, only grazing away from it for the minimum amount of time. Certainly animals know more than we realise. I trust that Erna and her friend are now enjoying the horses' Valhalla, having the hunting they both loved.

In 1972 I fell in love with Colligan Lodge near Dungarvon in County Waterford. My horses and I are now very happy living in this beautiful place with its ghosts, its peace and tranquillity, and its 'many, many trees'.